Thomas Merton

Introductions East & West

Thomas

INTRODUCTIONS

Edited by Robert E. Daggy

FOREWORD BY HARRY JAMES CARGAS

Greensboro:

Merton

EAST & WEST

The Foreign Prefaces of Thomas Merton

Unicorn Press, Inc.

ACKNOWLEDGMENTS

The editor and publisher gratefully acknowledge the original publication of the various prefaces included in this collection: preface to the French edition of EXILE ENDS IN GLORY (Copyright © 1955, Abbey of Gethsemani); preface to the French edition of MARTHA, MARY AND LAZARUS (Copyright © 1956, Desclée de Brouwer); preface to the French edition of THE ASCENT TO TRUTH (Copyright © 1958, Editions Albin Michel); preface to Argentinian edition of THE COMPLETE WORKS OF THOMAS MERTON (Copyright © 1960, Editorial Sudamericana); preface to the Japanese edition of THE SEVEN STOREY MOUNTAIN (Copyright © 1964, 1966, Abbey of Gethsemani); preface to the French edition of THE BLACK REVOLUTION (Copyright © 1964, Abbey of Gethsemani and Casterman, Inc.); preface to the Japanese edition of SEEDS OF CONTEMPLATION (Copyright © 1965, Abbey of Gethsemani; Copyright © 1968, University of Notre Dame Press); preface to the Korean edition of LIFE AND HOLINESS (Copyright © 1965, Abbey of Gethsemani and Kaetoric Chulpansha); preface to the Spanish edition of SEEDS OF DESTRUCTION (Copyright © 1965, Abbey of Gethsemani; Copyright © 1966, Editorial Pomaire); preface to the Japanese edition of THOUGHTS IN SOLITUDE (Copyright © 1966, Abbey of Gethsemani and Veritas Publishing Company; Copyright © 1966, Abbey of Gethsemani; Copyright © 1979, Trustees of the Thomas Merton Legacy Trust); preface to the Vietnamese edition of NO MAN IS AN ISLAND (Copyright © 1967, Abbey of Gethsemani; Copyright © 1971, 1980, Trustees of the Thomas Merton Legacy Trust); preface to the Japanese edition of THE NEW MAN (Copyright © 1970, Abbey of Gethsemani and Veritas Publishing Company; expanded version
(Copyright © 1979, Trustees of the Merton Legacy Trust).

Library of Congress Cataloging in Publication Data

Merton, Thomas, 1915-1968.
    Introductions east & west.

    Consists of the original prefaces, in English, which were translated into the various languages.
    "Checklist bibliography of Thomas Merton's major writings": p. 129.
    CONTENTS: Preface to the French edition of Exile ends in glory. — Preface to the French edition of Martha, Mary, and Lazarus. — Preface to the French edition of The ascent to truth. — [etc.]
    1. Spiritual life—Catholic author—Essays. I. Daggy, Robert E. II. Title.
BX2350.2.M4496   248.4'82   80-29263
ISBN 0-87775-139-0
ISBN 0-87775-140-4 (pbk.)

Unicorn Press, Inc.
P.O. Box 3307
Greensboro, North Carolina 27402

Table of Contents

FOREWORD

Here we have a Preface to a group of prefaces, a concept Thomas Merton would have enjoyed. Merton could laugh. He had a healthy sense of humor. What this fully means is that he had a deep sense of perspective.

"Wholeness" is a key word here. Merton strove to be a complete person and he urged the same for us in his writings. That is what the saint labors for: wholeness. None of us can fulfill that quest in this life but, as Goethe says, it is not in *achieving* sanctity that we are saved (for that is impossible) but in striving to achieve sanctity. Reduced to even simpler terms, we need to earn the two words that Kurt Vonnegut, Jr., placed on the tombstone of one of his fictional characters: *He tried.*

This attempt at wholeness, this striving, does not imply frantic action, flailing towards faith. Such action is one dimensional, a caricature—a cartoon where a masterpiece is required. Each of us paints our lives in different ways. For Merton, the best way to live was *apparently* to withdraw from life. For you and me the answer, he tells us, is different. But it is all part of the same answer, we read in the preface to the Argentine edition of his complete works. We must all make the effort together, "I with my books and prayers, you with your work and prayers. Separately we are incomplete. Together we are strong with the strength of God."

The unity of the human race—that is axiomatic for Merton as it must be for anyone adopting a monastic existence. To *escape* to a monastery is a kind of betrayal of the world, an abdication of one's humanity. To enter the secluded life for fulfillment—and that means in relation to all of humankind as well as to God—is a true vocation. The communal aspect of Christian holiness is important, Merton writes in his prefatory remarks to the Korean translation of *Life and Holiness.* And so the monk withdraws in order that he may be more with us. He leaves the world to serve it better.

1

Every person's holiness (just as every individual's sinfulness) affects me. A major message, Merton indicates in the fourth of his entries here, is that contemplative life applies wherever there is life. Or to put it another way, as he does in *Thoughts in Solitude* (preface to the Japanese edition), solitude is the ground of our being. We read earlier that "without contemplation we cannot see what we do in our apostolate. Without contemplation we cannot understand the significance of the world in which we must act."

Merton told us a great deal, but his life in fact was dedicated to listening. In telling, he shared with us what he heard. He knew that prayer is listening to God. In that way we develop not our individuality but our personality. I am unique, Merton wants me to know, but unique within a totality, not set apart from the whole. With my uniqueness goes a burden—What must I do with this gift? The answer goes something like this: I must become free. But as he says in the Japanese issue of *Seven Storey Mountain*, the only true liberty is to serve God.

Who knows best how I am to serve God? Certainly I don't. But the Creator of the universe does. God has a particular message for me. It is up to me to listen, to hear, then to act upon that continuing communication. And again, as Merton teaches (see the preface to the Japanese edition of *Seeds of Contemplation*), this action is not frantic, flailing, purposeless, self-deceiving. Order, peace and sanity all depend on the contemplative attitude, the solitude which a world of noise, violence, hatred, greed attempts to deny us.

Solitude now is not our natural condition. We have to struggle to earn it. In doing so we need God's help and we need the assistance of others who have heard their own individual messages and abstract the significance for us. These others are true teachers and Thomas Merton was (is) such a teacher. Every time we open a book of his we must read—and listen. This volume is no exception.

Harry James Cargas

INTRODUCTION

This collection, Introductions East and West: The Foreign Prefaces of Thomas Merton, *is a small portion of the literary legacy Merton left the world when he died in 1968. His bequest demonstrates the unusual scope of his literary accomplishments during his relatively brief career. Poet and essayist, biographer and critic, translator and diarist, novelist, autobiographer, sometime satirist, he was also a letter writer of extraordinary ability. He seemed — deceptively, perhaps, as it involved more work, thought and time than is apparent — to move easily from one form to another. His fluent style (he often said that he wrote "slang"), his lack of obscurity or pedantry, combine to conceal the fact that Thomas Merton was a careful and methodical writer who worked consistently to fulfill his commitment and vocation. He left an invaluable record in his papers of this working process, from which it is possible to recreate how, when and why he wrote most of his opus.*

Whether for his own use, from a sense of destiny, or through the scholarly process itself, Merton preserved (not always neatly!) most of the notes for and drafts of his finished writings. He also took detailed notes on his reading, usually dating them so that one can retrace in time the particular influences on him. Extensive marginal notes that he made in the books themselves, fortunately collected at the Abbey of Gethsemani and now transferred to the Thomas Merton Studies Center of Bellarmine College in Louisville, Kentucky, are another part of his legacy to us, as are the carbon copies he made of most of the drafts of his typescripts and of his letters.

Merton constantly sought precision in communication. He searched for the exact word or phrase, the additional sentence or paragraph, with which to clarify his meaning. Nearly everything he wrote was revised, and revised again, before he felt a work was finished. Even after an essay or article was published in a periodical or journal, he often revised it still again before permitting its inclusion in a collection; these typescripts, too, contain changes and additions. Nor did he stop here: he continued, as the

3

galleys of his books indicate, to change and polish up to the moment of publication. His practice of revising at different stages with different colored inks shows how many revisions he may have made in a single text. Most of his drafts, having been dated, can be arranged sequentially.

Merton scholarship has barely recognized these numerous versions, two or three of which may actually have been published; his bibliography is a maze of recurring and variant titles. It might seem on the surface that his prolificacy, though astounding, was neither so great nor so extensive as bibliographic listings indicate. However, his writing habits added a further dimension, since even materials with the same titles or themes often contain significantly varying passages and phrases. Few works, even after initial publication, were shelved. These foreign prefaces are an example of the process of revision and thought which characterized Merton as a writer. He did more than merely introduce a book to an audience outside the United States or, in some instances, to a people outside the mainstream of the Christian tradition. He reflected on his work and augmented the emphasis of his books as his own thoughts on them expanded. These prefaces represent Merton's thinking about his own books, thinking as he usually did — openly, honestly and with few illusions.

Time in which to think retrospectively about his books was limited for Merton. His active career as an author spanned only twenty years — from the publication of The Seven Storey Mountain *to his death. Despite his penchant for revising prior to publication, few of his published books received standard revision when they went into second or third printings, as few had been tested sufficiently by time or perspective to indicate the direction of possible revision. Thus, though Merton tirelessly revised his shorter pieces, he revised only one book-length work after publication and added almost no new prefaces to the American editions. The one book revised was* Seeds of Contemplation; *originally published in 1948, it appeared with new material and a new preface, in altered format, in 1962 as* New Seeds of Contemplation, *which he called "a completely new book."*

That Merton, in the two decades between 1948 and 1968, was able to reflect on his published work while writing a remarkable quantity of new material is indicative of his essentially contemplative life. These reflections have resulted in a complete record, through his revisions in his essays, of the development of his thinking.

In addition, he left a graph — now a valuable document — in which he evaluated his own books; this was drawn up in 1967 in response to a request for use in a class at Bellarmine College. Rather than using a more cursive format, Merton placed each of his major books on the graph, using a scale from "Awful" to "Best." Though it must be used carefully and contextually, the graph is important as his own assessment of his books. Between 1953 and 1967 he wrote ten special prefaces for translations of these books. Since, as noted, he wrote very little new prefatory material for American editions, these foreign prefaces represent his thinking on his books after publication and circulation. In some cases, they are his last printed statement on a particular book.

Merton tells us in these prefaces, which vary in quality and in length, about books he did not especially like once they were written. He tells us he might have written his autobiography differently had he written it later. He tells us he does not know quite how to address a people at war, a people with whom he feels intense sympathy but to whom he can offer little solace. He lets us see him thinking about the themes in the books he is introducing. In his attempts to convey aspects of Western idealism to the East, we glimpse his hopes for understanding between peoples. He conveys to us both the exhilaration and anguish which a monk, removed from the world, feels as he observes that world. Though the prefaces are not always the author at his best, he is direct, fresh, inventive, and always Merton. The prefaces are a unique part of the Merton corpus, and essential for future scholarship and criticism.

This collection was generated almost spontaneously in the Thomas Merton Studies Center, the repository designated by him for his papers. The prefaces came to my attention soon after I assumed the curatorship in 1974. Scholars and others requested information about them, primarily about the three published by Merton in his lifetime, those for the Japanese editions of The Seven Storey Mountain, Seeds of Contemplation, *and* Thoughts in Solitude. *One other, that for the Vietnamese edition of* No Man is an Island, *has been published in the United States, included in the posthumous collection* Thomas Merton on Peace, *printed in 1971.* Love and Living, *published in 1979, includes the preface for the Japanese edition of* The New Man *reworked considerably by Merton before his death. The preface for the Japanese edition of* The Seven Storey Moun-tain *was hard to find since it appeared in a journal with limited circula-tion. Those which had not been published in English were either unknown to American readers or impossible to obtain. Fortunately all existed in the translated editions at the Thomas Merton Studies Center and Merton's drafts for most of them had survived. I eventually compiled the prefaces with supporting material for use in the Center and for greater ease in responding to requests and answering questions.*

I have compared the various drafts and versions for this volume and, where possible, have chosen the text closest to that actually published abroad. I have included introductions to each preface for reference, infor-mation, and placement of the book and preface in the Merton career. Two additional items, Merton's graph evaluating his own books and a checklist bibliography, also prepared for use in the Center, are appended to the volume. I am grateful to several people for their aid and suggestions, especially to Brother Patrick Hart, O.C.S.O., of the Abbey of Gesth-emani; to Naomi Burton Stone, Trustee of the Thomas Merton Legacy Trust; to Debbie DiSalvo Heaverin, assistant in the Center who helped with the translation from the Spanish of the preface to the Argentine edition of The Complete Works of Thomas Merton; *to Teo Savory and Alan Brilliant of Unicorn Press for their encouragement, suggestions, and work; and to the Merton readers who made me aware of the value of these prefaces. Now, more than a decade after Merton's death in December, 1968, these prefaces, in addition to other works being published, demon-strate that his influence continues, his stature becomes universal.*

Robert E. Daggy

I

Preface to the French Edition

of

EXILE ENDS IN GLORY

July 1953

L'EXIL S'ACHÈVE DANS LA GLOIRE

PAR

THOMAS MERTON

DESCLÉE DE BROUWER

Thomas Merton first wrote a preface for a translation of one of his books in 1953. He wrote it for the French edition of Exile Ends in Glory, *the life of Mother M.* Berchmans, Trappistine missionary to Japan, published in the United States in June 1948 just four months before the publication of his phenomenally successful autobiography, The Seven Storey Mountain. *Unlike later prefaces to a book, which elaborated material already used, or which occasionally emerged as separate essays in their own right, this preface for* Exile Ends in Glory *was short and was, in Merton's words, an "apology." Merton was never quite satisfied with this book nor with his other hagiography,* What are these Wounds?, *life of Saint Lutgarde of Aywières.* What are these Wounds? *appeared two years after* Exile Ends in Glory *in the United States but two years before it in France. This preface is really an apology for both.*

The reasons for Merton's dissatisfaction are complex. He felt that both were poorly written. In his 1967 evaluation of his own books, he rated What are these Wounds? *"awful" and* Exile Ends in Glory *"bad." These were the only two books to which he gave these low ratings. They seemingly embarrassed Merton after other books, including* The Seven Storey Mountain, *brought him recognition as a writer of more than usual facility. That he felt he had been compelled to write these two biographies while still a novice continued to bother him. And he came to feel that they were written and conceived within a somewhat narrow religious framework. He later regretted that "not much ecumenical spirit" showed in* Exile Ends in Glory *and in 1964 urged that an Indonesian translation, which was never published, "suppress" several passages.*

Thus Merton wrote this first of his foreign prefaces to explain why he had written a book he considered bad, a book which he felt needed revision but which he never revised nor seemed to want to revise. No English drafts of the preface have survived and there are strong suggestions that Merton may have written it in French especially for this edition. This version was translated from the French by the editor who made no attempt to imitate or duplicate Merton's style. The preface appeared in none of the other translations of Exile Ends in Glory. *The French edition, published in Paris in 1955, contains Merton's definitive statement on a book which he considered a "pious memoir," a book which he says he thought, and which he hints he hoped, would remain anonymous.*

This book may possibly require an apology or at least an explanation. With its predecessor, WHAT ARE THESE WOUNDS?, it was written when the author was completing his novitiate. Except for a collection of the lives of saints, written toward the end of this period, which was not published, these were the first prose works which he wrote in the monastery.

When the author received the obedience from his superiors to write the biography of Mother Berchmans, he tried to adopt the literary style used in monasteries and convents, thinking he would write a book suitable for reading in a Trappist refectory. Convinced that the book would remain anonymous and would attract hardly any attention, he attempted to write a pious memoir similar to other pious memoirs.

But, once the work of the book was underway, the author found himself with a problem. To do justice to the saintliness of Mother Berchmans — which was certainly authentic and profound — it became necessary to rewrite the biography and even to do so in a different style. For several reasons this was impossible.

Fortunately the translator of the book, a Carmelite nun, was more than willing to play the role of editor and proof reader and the present version of the text is due to her untiring efforts. She assumed the task of revision, in order to make the work more accessible to a European public, and searched, in the documents which were our source of information, for new elements which would make the physiognomy of Mother Berchmans more exact and more vivid. For that, and for her patience with the impossibility of help from him, the author extends his thanks. Gratitude is due also to the Trappistines of Laval who generously offered to read the translation and who made numerous and valuable remarks.

The zeal and charity of all those who cooperated in the publication of this work contributed, over all, to its final success. We only hope that, in making available the life of a humble Trappistine contemplative, we have added another testimony to the essential apostolic character of all Christian life and, particularly, of contemplative life which cannot exist without our speaking at the same time with eloquence, even with silence, of the mystery of Christ.

II

Preface to the
French Edition
of
MARTHA, MARY
AND LAZARUS
April 1954

PRÉSENCE CHRÉTIENNE

Thomas Merton

MARTHE, MARIE et LAZARE

DESCLÉE DE BROUWER

Thomas Merton dealt extensively with the great Cistercian saint, Bernard of Clairvaux, in his work, in his thought, and in his lectures and classes to novices. By the mid 1950s he had done considerable research and work on St. Bernard and his writings.

He had written a series, "The Transforming Union in St. Bernard and St. John of the Cross," published in Collectanea Ordinis Cisterciensium Reformatorum *in the late 40s. In 1952 he wrote a special preface for a French biography of Bernard published in commemoration of his eighth centenary, and this preface was reprinted several times in English as "Saint Bernard, Monk and Apostle." One of two longer studies, originally called "The Life, Works and Doctrine of St. Bernard," which included Pope Pius XII's encyclical letter on Bernard's octocentennial, appeared in 1954 as* The Last of the Fathers. *This more scholarly work enjoyed limited success in the United States and eventually was translated only into French, Portuguese, and Spanish. Another study of St. Bernard, titled in draft "Action and Contemplation in the Doctrine of Saint Bernard," was partially published in three instalments of* Collectanea *in 1953. Merton reworked it into book form, added a preface, and retitled it* Martha, Mary and Lazarus.

The preface is unique in this volume since it was not intended to introduce a translation but a possible English publication. It has appeared, however, despite various projects for publication, only in translation. It appeared initially in the 1956 French edition Marthe, Marie et Lazare, *published by Desclée de Brouwer as part of their "Présence chrétienne" series. The only other edition of this Merton work has been the Portuguese translation from the French,* Marta, Maria e Lazaro, *which was published in Brazil in 1963.*

It is impossible to understand any aspects of the doctrine of Saint Bernard if we do not see this doctrine as a whole from the beginning, just as we cannot penetrate the real sense if, from the outset, the Spirit of the One who speaks to us through the works of Saint Bernard is not present. Bernard of Clairvaux is above all a "man of the Church" — *vir Ecclesiae*. Like the Evangelists, like Paul and John, Saint Gregory the Great and Saint Augustine, Saint Maximus the Confessor and Cassian, who preceded him, and especially Saint Benedict, his spiritual father, Bernard uniquely grasped all aspects of the spiritual life in their relation to the great essential mystery, without which they make no sense. This mystery is the very essence of Christianity — it is Christ Himself: the Christ manifest of the Father, the beginning and the end of all, the One in whom all things subsist and in whom all things in heaven and on earth find their end, their accomplishment, their final significance.[1] To see all things "in Christ" is to see them in Christ complete, in the mystic person in whom the Head is completed by its members and in whom the members complete themselves and complete the Head. Saint Bernard saw all these as central to the mystery of the Church.

If then the contemplative life holds a special place in the doctrine of Saint Bernard and the teachings of those who preceded him, it is because contemplation alone makes completely clear our union with Christ, the union of our life in Him and of His life in us. Contemplation is the achievement in each member of the Church of the mystic union which binds Christ to His Church, expressed by Him as marriage.

Saint Bernard took the *Song of Songs* as the theme for a series of mystic sermons because the book seemed to him most appropriate for serving the spiritual nourishment of the monks. It completes the ascetic teaching of the other Books of Wisdom.[2] It enables the monks, already striving for perfection and growth in Christ, to recognize, in the songs they sing, in the unfathomable depths of their very hearts, union with the Word in perfect charity.[3] But, at

[1] Colossians 1:17.
[2] Sermon I *in Cantica*, n. 2-3. M.P.L. 183. 785.
[3] Serm. I *in Cantica*, n. 11-12, 789.

the same time, it reminds them that espousal of the Word bears fruit in the apostolic life.

Our present task is to study the relationship among action, contemplation, and the apostolic life in the doctrine of Saint Bernard. The necessity of this study to us is unquestionable. As happens with Saint Thomas Aquinas — who treats the same subject from a different point of view — Saint Bernard is frequently quoted out of context, either partially or incompletely. Extracts from the Abbey of Clairvaux are sometimes presented in a way supporting the principle of contemplation, sometimes that of apostolic life. And we often find these citations, lifted out of context and out of the unity of Saint Bernard's thought, contradictory. For example, we easily understand what the Saint was saying when he spoke of the soul's desire to be the vehicle of grace before having gained, through contemplation, sufficient reserves of charity to nourish the apostolic life.[4] On the other hand, the supporters of the apostolic life quickly point out that Saint Bernard has said we should give priority to the apostolic life rather than to the repose of contemplative life. The milk of apostolic teaching, with which we nourish babes in Christ, is "more necessary" than the wine of contemplation which delights our hearts: *Ubera quibus parvulos alis, meliora, hoc est necessariora, sunt vino contemplationis.*[5]

What does this mean? It is evident that both sides are right since both statements are part of the authentic teaching of Saint Bernard. The purpose of this book is simply to reconcile these two points of view and to show how, in the thought of Saint Bernard, the apostolate represents an absolute necessity and obligation, in certain precise circumstances, preferable to contemplation. However, apostolic life without contemplation is sterile. That is why the value of apostolic life is *largely* a function of the contemplative source. This doctrine is neither new nor strange; it represents the traditional teaching of the Church.

We would make a serious error if we approached this question

---

[4] "Canales hodie in Ecclesia multos habemus, conchas perpaucas . . ." etc. Serm. 18 *in Cantica*, n. 3. M.P.L. 183. 860.
[5] Serm. 9 *in Cantica*, n. 8. M.P.L. 183. 818.

without defining our terms. Saint Bernard does not use words referring to the active life and the contemplative life at all in the sense which we use them today. Actually the arguments favoring the active life as opposed to the contemplative life tend to be a comparison between the life of active *religious orders* and that of *contemplative orders*. Saint Bernard had no interest in that question. No such lines were drawn for him. On the contrary, he considered action, contemplation and the apostolic life as equal functions within the monastery itself, each of these "vocations" was part of the properly defined monastic vocation. Martha and Mary were not rivals; they were sisters. Their abodes were not separate; they did not cavil to know which would receive the Lord Jesus under her roof since they lived in the same house and Jesus visited them both at the same time. If they disagreed, it was due to Martha's failure to understand why Mary did not take a more active part in a life which, on the whole, they shared. It is clear that action and contemplation — as Saint Bernard understands them — are simply two parts of the monastic life: *Sunt invicem contubernales hae duae, et cohabitant pariter; est quippe soror Mariae Martha.*[6]

Here again we need to be careful. Exactly what did Saint Bernard mean by active life and contemplative life? In our time, when we see all things from the outside rather than apprehending them from within, when we judge on appearance rather than from the heart, we think that it is enough to stress the cloister to distinguish contemplative life and active life. Contemplative life leads one behind a wall, into the cloister; active life leads one out of the enclosure, into public places. According to this simplistic view, contemplative life is defined by the absence of active work. Contemplative orders should be those who do not preach, who do not teach, who do not run hospitals. Yes, but what do they do? In order to give the contemplative orders a special activity, we say that their dynamic lies in prayer. Active orders preach to the world; contemplative orders pray for the world. In this way the religious life is divided into two camps, each given its own brand of activity. On the one hand we have an exterior and public activity; on the other a hidden and interior activity, but not an interior

[6] Serm. 50 *in Cantica*, n. 2. M.P.L. 183. 1026.

activity sufficient nonetheless without manifesting itself outwardly in a great number of complicated exercises. In short, we distinguish the active religious life and the contemplative religious life, not by showing what they are, but simply by indicating what they are not: not by showing what they may be, but only by showing what they have been.

Remember once more that this distinction would have seemed strange to Saint Bernard, just as it would have to the other Church Fathers. As we have seen, Saint Bernard found it natural that the vocations of active life and contemplative life should exist in the confines of the same monastery. In general, all should pray together behind the same enclosure, all should work together and read together in the cloister. Their exterior occupations should be approximately the same. It is true that the monk, charged with a special function in connection with the exterior life (*officialis frater*) may have a particular task, such as steward, or infirmarian, or gatekeeper. But we have also come to see that active life within a monastery may be a purely interior attitude. Two monks, standing side by side in choir, singing the same psalms when seated together in the cloister, or working together in the fields, doing the same thing all day, will each inevitably lead a different life, due to the difference in their interior dispositions. For one it may be the contemplative life of Mary, for another the active and penitential life of Lazarus, or, if he is charged with tasks and material cares, the life of the diligent Martha.

It is quite evident that living in a monastery does not at all divert a contemplative. When Saint Bernard tells us of the contemplative life, he means by it something profound and real. He means a life of close union with God in mystic prayer: the life of *Sponsa Verbi*, embraced by the monk not only as his condition but as his interior choice.

All monks are not contemplatives. Some lead an active life, in the sense that their "spirit" is active, an activity geared toward penitence. Others are active because they are concerned with numerous tasks for the good of the community. And finally others are active in the apostolic sense: particularly the superiors and those whose mission it is to direct and form the other monks. In

the thought of Saint Bernard, only the Abbey Fathers seemed to fit into this category.

But how does one choose a vocation to active life or to contemplative life? If we understand completely the term "contemplative life," if we mean by that a life where all is cast in a superior plan of mystic grace, then such a vocation is a gratuitous gift which God accords us. We can neither attain it nor possess it by ourselves, but we can desire it. That then brings us to the most important point of our study. Saint Bernard tells us in so many words that we can always orient our desires and our efforts in one or the other of these two directions. We can tend toward an active life or toward a contemplative life. Remember that, on this subject, asceticism has always been considered by the Church Fathers as a normal preparation for contemplative prayer. But which, all things considered, should be the chief object of our aspirations? Saint Bernard does not hesitate to give us an answer: in the case where the monk is free to choose among the three lives: active, apostolic and contemplative, and in the case where he is disposed to choose, he should always prefer the vocation of Mary: *Pars ipsa Mariae, quantum in nobis est, est omnibus eligenda.* [7]

This, as is well known, is in perfect accord with the true monastic spirit. For a real monk, who arrives at the cloister actually "en cherchant réellement Dieu," as Saint Benedict expressed it, it is certain that he is less concerned with working for God than in finding Him, knowing Him, possessing Him and being possessed by Him.

The mystery of Divine selection subsists and, more than that, it is true that many are called and few chosen. However, certainly the monk who is faithful to his vocation watches constantly with fixed eyes from "the eternal hill," while he lives always on the threshold of that other world. It matters little whether he ever attains perfect union with God on earth; it matters little whether he is active or contemplative, penitent or apostle, he will inevitably be a man of God and a man of prayer, else he will not be a monk.

---

[7] Serm. III *de Assumptione*, n. 3. M.P.L. 183. 422.

Saint Bernard wanted to proclaim this fundamental truth of the monastic life, remembering that his age debated whether what one does for God is less important than what one is, and whether to be a monk did not consist solely in working for God and in serving Him else one could not be a true son. In effect, the monk, by his angelic life, by his spiritual virginity, by his detachment from regard for earthly things, lives as a bridesmaid of the Divine Word who awaits her Bridegroom in the night, lamp at hand, ready to follow Him where He leads.

III

Preface to the

French Edition

of

THE ASCENT

TO TRUTH

November 1957

THOMAS MERTON

LA MONTÉE
VERS LA
LUMIÈRE

(THE ASCENT TO TRUTH)

traduit de l'américain par
MARIE TADIÉ

ÉDITIONS
ALBIN MICHEL

The Ascent to Truth, *published in September 1951 in the United States, was a more modest commercial success than Merton's earlier works,* The Seven Storey Mountain, Seeds of Contemplation, *and* The Waters of Siloe. *Merton indicated at various times that he was less than entirely satisfied with the book and he rated it "Fair" on a scale from "Awful" to "Best" on his 1967 evaluation graph. By November 1957 when he wrote the preface for the French edition, it had been translated and published only in Argentina, Belgium, Germany, and Italy, a far less impressive record than had occurred with* The Seven Storey Mountain, *and* Seeds of Contemplation. *A British edition appeared simultaneously with the American in 1951 and an American paperback edition, which went quickly out of print, in 1959. A Portuguese translation was published in Brazil and a second Spanish edition in Argentina, both in 1958 shortly after the publication of the French edition, but neither included the preface nor the revisions which had been made for the French version. A second British edition, issued in 1976, made this work available in English again.*

Merton called the French edition, as edited and cut by Father François de Ste. Marie, the final version. He made no attempt to revise or alter the 1959 paperback English language edition and the 1976 British edition is not a translation of the French "final" version. At this point that which Merton called the definitive version of The Ascent to Truth *is still unavailable in English.*

The French edition, La Montée vers la Lumière, *translated by Marie Tadié who translated most of Merton's books into French, was published in Paris in early 1958. Merton's original typescript from which this version was edited, now in the possession of Sr. M. Thérèse Lentfoehr, S.D.S., is dated "All Saints, 1957."*

This book is not intended to be a guide to the mystical life, or a synthesis of contemplative spirituality, or anything of the sort. It is rather an informal and meditative study of one particular aspect of the interior life—the relation between knowledge and love, the intelligence and the will, in the quest for God. Moreover, the study is restricted still further by the fact that it is limited more or less to the teaching of St. Thomas Aquinas and St. John of the Cross on this particular question. Such an approach obviously has its limitations as well as its advantages. Among the advantages we may cite simplicity and clarity, and among the limitations perhaps a certain restriction of perspective and a consequent danger of misunderstanding.

Thus, for example, if much is said about "reason" in the earlier chapters, it is taken for granted that the reader understands that our attention is being focused on a very special aspect of the interior life, and that the author has no intention of preaching a sort of rationalistic and pelagian variety of interior prayer. If it is true that grace builds upon nature, then it is evident that grace makes use of the natural faculties of man in order to bring him to God, and the two faculties which play the most important part in man's interior life are his intelligence and his will. But obviously again, it is not by the action of these faculties that man arrives at union with God, but by divine grace. Man cannot divinize himself. He can only be divinized by the Holy Spirit—and that means that our way to God is a way of submission to Him Whom we do not see and never fully understand. Nevertheless, as this book will show in some detail, our very submission to grace is reasonable, and we cannot cooperate with God as he intends us to unless our cooperation is intelligent and enlightened by His divine light. Intelligence is therefore most important in the interior life, but there is something more important still and that is love.

One cannot discuss, in detail, man's knowledge and love of God without seeming to take a rather psychological and ethical view of the interior life. This in turn has the disadvantage of encouraging a certain inordinate subjectivism, a constant tendency to observe one's own reactions, which can have unfortunate consequences. It is assumed that the reader will be able to regain his perspective by remembering that this is only a very partial and limited kind of study, and that which is said here is by no means the whole story.

This book was written seven years ago. If I were to attack the same subject at the present day (and I very probably would not), I might approach it very differently. For one thing, the psychological aspects of the study would have to be completed by some discussion of man's unconscious drives and their possible intervention in the life of prayer. On the other hand, I would prefer to draw more upon Scripture and the Fathers and to concern myself a little less with scholasticism which is not the true intellectual climate for a monk. In a word, the book would be quite different from what it actually is.

When the question of the French edition was brought up, I at first thought of making extensive revisions. This was not only impossible but useless. Instead, the French translation has been very carefully edited, by Père François de Ste. Marie, O.C.D. Extensive digressions have been cut out. The important passages have been simplified and clarified, and less important ones have been suppressed. I myself have gone over the manuscript and made further cuts, and introduced a few revisions. As a result, the book now stands in definitive form, and the French edition henceforth replaces all others (including the English) as the final version. It contains all that the author desires to retain of the original. The rest can profitably be forgotten.

This result could not have been achieved without the generous help of Père François de Ste. Marie and the untiring patience of Marie Tadié who has worked harder and longer on this difficult translation than on any other she has done for me.

IV

Preface to the

Argentine Edition

of

THE COMPLETE

WORKS OF

THOMAS MERTON

April 1958

THOMAS MERTON
(fr. M. Louis, O.C.S.O.)

OBRAS COMPLETAS

I

LA MONTAÑA DE LOS SIETE CÍRCULOS

SEMILLAS DE CONTEMPLACIÓN

LAS AGUAS DE SILOÉ

EL EXILIO Y LA GLORIA

¿QUÉ LLAGAS SON ÉSAS?

LA SENDA DE LA CONTEMPLACIÓN

PAN EN EL DESIERTO

EDITORIAL SUDAMERICANA
BUENOS AIRES

In 1958, ten years after the publication of The Seven Storey Mountain, *Thomas Merton had published over thirty major books and pamphlets
and dozens of articles. In that year Editorial Sudamericana in Buenos
Aires approached him with a project to issue a definitive and open-ended
series of his books to be called "The Complete Works of Thomas Merton."
Fifteen major Merton items had been translated into Spanish, published by
houses in Spain, Chile, Argentina, and Mexico, and distributed throughout the Spanish speaking world. Ten had been published by Sudamericana
and the firm, convinced of Merton's continued commercial viability, proposed to collect seven early works into a deluxe one volume edition instead of
releasing second editions individually.*

*The volume as projected, and as eventually completed, contained the
full-length* The Seven Storey Mountain, Seeds of Contemplation,
The Waters of Siloe, Exile Ends in Glory, What are these
Wounds?, *and* Bread in the Wilderness. *Sudamericana also obtained
the rights for inclusion of a composite of shorter pieces, "Self-denial and the
Christian," "A Balanced Life of Prayer," "Poetry and Contemplation,"
and "What is Contemplation?", published under the title* The Way of
Contemplation *by Rialp in Madrid. This volume had gone into a second
printing by 1958. Sudamericana omitted their other three Merton titles,*
The Ascent to Truth, No Man is an Island, *and* The Silent Life,
*all in print and selling, from this project with the assumption that they
could provide the base for a second volume of Collected Works. Merton
approved the project and was pleased with the opportunity to write a
preface intended especially for Latin American readers. It was the only new
preface he wrote for a Spanish language edition.*

*The volume. handsomely bound and impressively weighty, appeared in
1960 with the title* Obras Completas I. *Sudamericana failed to continue
the series and published no* Obras Completas II, *although nineteen more
Merton works have been translated into Spanish. They had, in fact,
already printed a second edition of* The Ascent to Truth *in individual
volume before 1960. This project, however, remains the only attempt,
incomplete as it has been, to collect the Merton corpus in a series.*

*Merton's English draft has not survived. There are strong suggestions
that he may have written the draft in Spanish with the aid of Spanish
speaking novices then at the Abbey of Gethsemani. This translation from
the printed Argentine edition was made by this editor. He was assisted by
Debbie DiSalvo Heaverin, assistant to the Curator, Thomas Merton
Studies Center. The translation is more or less literal and there has been no
attempt to imitate Merton's inimitable style.*

I am honored to see, before such an edition should appear elsewhere, the publication of my "Complete Works" in South America. I find this significant and I think it demands very special recognition from me.

Those who read the first pages of this volume will be aware that I am one of millions whose destiny brought him from the shores of Europe to become a citizen of the Western hemisphere, a man of the New World. I actually already belonged to the New World in a sense since my mother's family had lived there for several generations. I came seeking an answer to the inscrutable problems of life and found an answer both old and new—an answer pertaining to no time, country, continent or culture. I found the word of salvation in the New World. I also found a paradoxical vocation for the contemplative life—a vocation incomprehensible to some, as if the contemplative life is confined to the Old World which is dying rather than to the New World which is being born.

I believe the major message in these pages is that the contemplative life applies wherever there is life. Wherever man and society exist; where there are hopes, ideals, aspirations for a better future; where there is love—and where there is mingled pain and happiness—there the contemplative life has a place, because life, happiness, pain, ideals, aspirations, work, art and other things have significance. If these things have no significance, why waste our time on them? But, if they have significance, then the independent signficance of each must converge in some way into a central and universal significance which comes from a hidden reality. This central reality has to be a "catholic" reality, a "divine" reality. The reality central to my life is the life of God. To know this is the contemplative's objective.

In my case, the word of salvation, the gospel of Jesus Christ, has led me to solitude and to silence. My vocation is rare perhaps, but contemplation does not exist only within the walls of the cloister. Every man, to live a life full of significance, is called simply to know the significant interior of life and to find ultimate significance in its proper inscrutable existence, in spite of himself, in spite of the world and appearances, in the Living God. Every man born on this earth is called to find and realize himself in Christ and, through Him, to comprehend the unity of Christ with all men, so much so that he loves them as they love themselves and is one with them almost as he is one with himself: then the spirit of Christ is one with those who love Him.

In the silence of the countryside and the forest, in the cloistered solitude of my monastery, I have discovered the whole Western Hemisphere. Here I have been able, through the grace of God, to explore the New World, without traveling from city to city, without flying over the Andes or the Amazon, stopping one day here, two there, and then continuing on. Perhaps if I had traveled in this manner, I should have seen nothing: generally those who travel most see the least.

It seems that I have heard the voice of all the hemisphere in the silence of my monastery, a voice that speaks from the depths of my being with a clarity at once magnificent and terrible: as if I had in my heart the vast and solitary pampas, the brilliant hoarfrost of the Bolivian plateau, the thin air of the terraced valleys of the Incas, the splendor and suavity of Quito, the cold plains of Bogotá, and the mysterious jungles of the Amazon. It seems that entire cities with great opulence and terrible indigence side by side live inside me. It seems that the ancient civilizations of Mexico, older even than Egypt, gather in unspeakable silence in my heart. It seems that I hear in the even more profound silence of Peru the forgotten syllables of ancient wisdom which has never died and which contains in its secrets an image of truth that no man has recognized, an image, symbolic and prophetic, like that of Jesus Christ. It seems that the unending beauty of the New World with its limitless possibilities moves within me like a giant sleeper in whose presence I am unable to remain indifferent. In reality, it seems at times that this presence inside me speaks with the voice of God Himself; and I struggle vainly to grasp and to understand some word, some syllable of the destiny of the New World—the destiny that is still hidden in the mystery of Providence.

One thing I know—that it is my destiny to be a contemplative, a Christian, and an American. I can satisfy my vocation with nothing that is partial or provincial. I cannot be a "North American" who knows only the rivers, the plains, the mountains and the cities of the north, the north where there are few Indians, where the land was colonized and cultivated by the Puritans, where, under the audacious and sarcastic splendor of the skyscrapers, one rarely sees the Cross and where the Holy Virgin, when she is represented at all, is pale and melancholy and carries no child in her arms. This north is grand, powerful, rich, intelligent; it has a warmth of its own, a surprising humility, a charity, an inner purity which the stranger does not know. But it is incomplete. It is neither the better nor the richer part of the hemisphere. It is perhaps, at this point in time, the most important region of the world, but it is, nonetheless, not sufficient in itself and it lacks fundamental roots. It lacks the roots of the old America, the America of Mexico and the Andes, where silent and contemplative Asians came, milleniums ago, to construct their hieratic cities. It lacks the intense fervor and fecundity of Brazil, which is also African, which smiles with the grin of the Congo and laughs with the childlike innocence of Portugal. The northern half of this New World lacks the force, the refinement, the prodigality of Argentina with all the lyricism of its tormented and generous heart.

I cannot be a partial American and I cannot be, which is even sadder, a partial Catholic. For me Catholicism is not confined to one culture, one nation, one age, one race. My faith is not a mixture of the Irish Catholicism of the United States and the splendid and vital Catholicism, reborn during the past war, of my native France. Though I admire the cathedrals and the past of Catholicism in Latin America, my Catholicism goes beyond the Spanish tradition. I cannot believe that Catholicism is tied to the destinies of any group which confusedly expresses the economic illusions of a social class. My Catholicism is not the religion of the bourgeoisie nor will it ever be. My Catholicism is all the world and all ages. It dates from the beginning of the world. The first man was the image of Christ and contained Christ, even as he was created, as savior in his heart. The first man was destined to be the ancestor of his Redeemer and the first woman was the mother of all life, in the image of the Immaculate Daughter who was full of grace, Mother of mercy, Mother of the saved.

This Holy Mother is the Mother of America—she is in all parts of America, *la Virgen Morena!* [1] Her banner was in the vanguard of the armies of American independence. She is in all parts of America, particularly in Spanish America, and there she embodies, in her mystery, the Body of Christ.

For many in our New World, the Church is merely a respectable institution closely linked to a past society. This is a grave mistake and a disastrous error—an error which we clergy and religious must try to dissipate, not only with our teaching, but also with our lives. We love our old traditions, but we are men of the future. Our responsibility is to the future, not to the past. The past does not depend on us, but the future does. Certainly we ought, like our Master, to say that "our happiness is not of this world," and we have to understand that what we do to the humblest of His creation, we do to Him; part of our work for the salvation of mankind must be to construct a world in which man can willingly prepare for God—with vision of a free life on earth.

The Church in this New World is more than a decorative symbol of the past. It is the mother of the future. Its members must open their eyes to the future; they must recognize the signs that point to the future, signs through which God Himself speaks in the obscurity of history and in the present activity and life of the surrounding world. This is what the modern fathers have told us, calling us to "Catholic" action, asking for new orientation in our vocation for the priesthood in the New World. This orientation, however, depends on very old traditions which the modern world has forgotten and only recently has begun to remember: the priority of spirituality and the primacy of contemplation.

Contemplation cannot construct a new world by itself. Contemplation does not feed the hungry; it does not clothe the naked; it does not teach the ignorant; and it does not return the sinner to peace, truth, and union with God. But without contemplation we cannot see what we do in our apostolate. Without contemplation we cannot understand the significance of the world in which we must act. Without contemplation we remain small, limited, divided, partial: we adhere to the insufficient, permanently united to our narrow group and its interests, losing sight of justice and charity, seized by the passions of the moment, and, finally, we betray Christ. Without contemplation, without the intimate, silent, secret pursuit of truth through love, our action loses itself in the world and becomes dangerous. Yet, if our contemplation is fanatic or false, our action becomes much more dangerous. We should lose ourselves to win the world; we should humble ourselves to find Christ everywhere and to love Him in all beings: instead, we betray Him by not seeing Him in those whom we harm unconsciously while we "innocently" pray for them.

The essence of the monastic rule is contained in these few words: "Preferring absolutely nothing to the love of Christ . . ." The new world is built with lasting standards by this love of Christ, the Christ in ourselves and the Christ in our fellow men. The new world will not be built by the Russian perversion of the Marxist dialectic. The new world will not be built by the destructive passions of Fascist militarism. The new world will not be built by the magic of imperialist technology. We cannot hope for anything more than deception and confusion in "dollar diplomacy." The western hemisphere is enormously rich, richer probably than the rest of the world. Its riches belong to those who live in Him, but shared exploitation of those riches and their just distribution will not solve our problem. It is basically the problem of man, a problem of comprehension and of love, a problem of unity. This is most important since man is made in the image of God, and until he is fully united with himself, with his brothers, and with his God, the reign of God cannot come and manifest itself on earth so that all may see His kingdom. And this can never be achieved except in Christ and through the power of the cross and the victory of His resurrection.

This, then, is what seems to me so important about America—and the great function of my vocation in it: to know America in its totality, to be a complete American, a man of the whole hemisphere, of the whole New World; to be a complete Christian, a complete contemplative, and through this, to help others to know Christ in the fullness of maturity, in all His universality, until we all attain to the unity of faith and of the deep knowledge of the Son of God, to perfect manhood, to the mature measure of the fullness of Christ; and this He has done that we may be now no longer children, tossed to and fro and carried about by every wind of doctrine devised in the wickedness of men, in craftiness, according to the wiles of error; rather are we to practise the truth in love, and so to grow up in all things in Him who is the head, Christ.

(Ephesians 4:13-15)[2]

God grant that those who read this book and I who wrote it will remain united in this ideal and in this struggle. We must work together as Americans and Christians, as brothers and as builders—I with my books and prayers, you with your work and prayers. Separately we are incomplete. Together we are strong with the strength of God. Oh, my brothers and sisters of the South, it makes me happy that this book reunites us in Christ; but the book is, after all, not really necessary: we are already one in our love of truth, our passion for freedom, and our adoration of the Living God.

V

Preface to the

Japanese Edition

of

THE

SEVEN STOREY

MOUNTAIN

August 1963

THOMAS

The Seven Storey Mountain

MERTON

七重の山

■トーマス・マートン著／工藤 貞訳／中央出版社

The Seven Storey Mountain, *published in the United States in October 1948, was the most successful of Thomas Merton's writings. By August 1963 when Merton wrote the preface to the Japanese edition, his first reflection on the book and the passing of time,* The Seven Storey Mountain *had gone through multiple printings in hardcover and paperback in the United States, had been edited by Evelyn Waugh and retitled* Elected Silence *in Great Britain, and had been published in translation in Argentina, Belgium, Brazil, Denmark, France, Germany, Italy, the Netherlands, Portugal, Spain (both Castilian and Catalan), and Sweden. Fifteen years after its initial publication (Merton calls it "nearly twenty years" since so much of his writing took place well before publication), he paused to comment on the one work whose appearance had made him an internationally known writer. The preface to the Japanese edition was the only "special" preface which Merton wrote for a later edition of* The Seven Storey Mountain, *a fact which makes this preface unique and significant.*

The Japanese edition, titled Nanae no Yama *and translated by Tadashi Kudo, was delayed in Japan through editorial problems. One page of the English text became four pages when translated into Japanese thus threatening a somewhat unwieldy finished product. This problem and others were eventually solved and the Japanese edition was finally published in Tokyo in 1966. By then Merton had already published the preface in English with the title "Introducing a Book." It appeared in the January 1964 issue of* Queen's Work, *printed verbatim from Merton's mimeographed version which itself had been circulated as usual by Merton among friends and religious houses.*

The text of The Seven Storey Mountain *was printed in Japanese in the edition, but Merton's preface, for some reason, was printed in English. Merton made some late changes in the text of the preface and discrepancies occur between the Japanese "English" version and the version printed as "Introducing a Book." These changes are indicated in the notes placed at the end of this book.*

Nearly twenty years have passed since this book was written. The occasion of a new preface invites the author to reflect once again on the story, his own story, and the way he has told it.

Perhaps if I were to attempt this book today, it would be written differently. Who knows? But it was written when I was still quite young, and that is the way it remains. The story no longer belongs to me, and I have no right to tell it in a different way, or to imagine that it should have been seen through wiser eyes. In its present form, which will remain its only form, it belongs to many people. The author no longer has an exclusive claim upon his story.

But if the story remains what it is, has the author changed?

Certainly I have never for a moment thought of changing the definitive decisions taken in the course of my life: to be a Christian, to be a monk, to be a priest. If anything, the decision to renounce and to depart from modern secular society, a decision repeated and reaffirmed many times, has finally become irrevocable. Yet the attitude and the assumptions behind this decision have perhaps changed in many ways.

For one thing, when I wrote this book, the fact uppermost in my mind was that I had seceded from the world of my time in all clarity and with total freedom. The break and the secession were, to me, matters of the greatest importance. Hence the somewhat negative tone of so many parts of this book.

Since that time, I have learned, I believe, to look back into that world with greater compassion, seeing those in it not as alien to myself, not as peculiar and deluded strangers, but as identified with myself. In breaking from "their world" I have strangely broken from them. In freeing myself from their delusions and preoccupations I have identified myself, none the less, with their struggles and their blind, desperate hope of happiness.

But precisely because I am identified with them, I must refuse all the more definitively to make their delusions my own. I must refuse their ideology of matter, power, quantity, movement, activism and force. I reject this because I see it to be the source[1] and the expression of the spiritual hell which man has made of his world: the hell which has burst into flame in two total wars of incredible horror, the hell of spiritual emptiness and sub-human

43

fury[2] which has resulted in crimes like Auschwitz and Hiroshima. This I can and must reject with all the power of my being. This all sane men seek to reject. But the question is: how can one sincerely reject the effect if he continues to embrace the cause?

My conversion to the Christian faith, or to be precise my conversion to Christ, is something I have always regarded as a radical liberation from the delusions and obsessions of modern man and his society. I have always believed and continue to believe that faith is the only real protection against the absorption of freedom and intelligence in the crass and thoughtless servitude of mass society. Religious faith, and faith alone, can open the inner ground of man's being to the liberty of the sons of God, and preserve him from the surrender of his integrity to the seduction of a totalitarian life.[3] The reason for this is that no matter what man thinks, his thought is based on a fundamental belief of some sort. If his belief is in slogans and doctrines which are foisted on him by a political or economic ideology, he will surrender his inmost truth to an exterior compulsion. If his belief is a suspension of belief, and an acceptance of physical stimulation for its own sake, he still continues to "believe" in the possibility of some rational happiness to be attained in this manner. Man must believe in something, and that in which he believes becomes his god. To serve some material or human entity as one's god is to be a slave of that which perishes, and thus to be a slave of death, sorrow, falsehood, misery. The only true liberty is in the service of that which is beyond all limits, beyond all definitions, beyond all human appreciation: that which is All, and which therefore is no limited or individual thing: the All is no-thing, for if it were to be a single thing separated from all other things, it would not be All. This precisely is the liberty I have always sought: the freedom of being subject to no-thing and therefore to live in All, through All, for All, by Him who is All. In Christian terms, this is to live "in Christ" and by the "Spirit of Christ," for the Spirit is like the wind, blowing where He pleases, and He is the Spirit of Truth. "The Truth shall make you free."

But if the Truth is to make me free, I must also let go my hold upon myself, and not retain the semblance of a self which is an object or a "thing." I too must be no-thing. And when I am no-thing, I am in the All, and Christ lives in me. But He who lives in me is in all those around me. He who lives in the chaotic world of men is hidden in the midst of them, unknowable and unrecognizable because he is no-thing. Thus in the cataclysms of our world, with its crimes, its lies and its fantastic violence, He who suffers in all is the All who still cannot suffer. Yet in us it is He who suffers, that we may live in Him.

Many rumors have been disseminated about me since I came to the monastery. Most of them have assured people that I had left the monastery, that I had returned to New York, that I was in Europe, that I was in South America or Asia, that I had become a hermit, that I was married, that I was drunk, that I was dead.

I am still in the monastery, and intend to stay there. I have never had any doubt whatever of my monastic vocation. If I have ever had any desire for change, it has been for a more solitary, more "monastic" way. But precisely because of this it can be said that I am in some sense everywhere. My monastery is not a home. It is not a place where I am rooted and established in the earth. It is not an environment in which I become aware of myself as an individual, but rather a place in which I disappear from the world as an object of interest in order to be everywhere in it by hiddenness and compassion. To exist everywhere I have to be No-one.

But the monastery is not an "escape" from the world. On the contrary, by being in the monastery I take my true part in all the struggles and sufferings of the world. To adopt a life that is essentially non-assertive, non-violent, a life of humility and peace is in itself a statement of one's position. But each one in such a life can, by the personal modality of his decision, give his whole life[4] a special orientation. It is my intention to make my entire life a rejection of, a protest against the crimes and injustices of war and political tyranny which threaten to destroy the whole race of man and the world with him. By my monastic life and vows I am saying NO to all the concentration camps, the aerial bombardments, the staged political trials, the judicial murders, the racial injustices, the economic tyrannies, and the whole socio-economic apparatus which seems geared for nothing but global destruction in spite of all its fair words in favor of peace. I make monastic silence a protest against the lies of politicians, propagandists and agitators, and when I speak it is to deny that my faith and my Church can ever seriously be aligned with these forces of injustice and destruction. But it is true, nevertheless, that the faith in which I believe is also invoked by many who believe in war, believe in racial injustices, believe in self-righteous and lying forms of tyranny. My life must, then, be a protest against these also, and perhaps against these most of all.

If there is a "problem" for Christianity today, it is the problem of the identification of "Christendom" with certain forms of culture and society, certain political and social structures which for fifteen-hundred years have dominated Europe and the West. The first monks were men who, already in the fourth century, began to protest against this identification as a falsehood and a servitude. Fifteen-hundred years of European Christendom, in spite of certain definite achievements, have not been an unequivocal glory for Christendom.[5] The time has come for judgment[6] to be passed on this history. I can rejoice in this fact, believing that the judgment will be a liberation of the Christian faith from servitude to and involvement in the structures of the secular world. And that is why I think certain forms of Christian "optimism" are to be taken with reservations, in so far as they lack the genuine eschatalogical consciousness of the Christian vision, and concentrate upon the naive hope of merely temporal achievements—churches on the moon!

If I say NO to all these secular forces, I also say YES to all that is good in the world and in man. I say YES to all that is beautiful in nature, and in order that this may be the yes of a[7] freedom and not of subjection, I must refuse to possess any thing in the world purely as my own. I say YES to all the men and women who are my brothers and sisters in the world, but for this yes to be an assent of freedom and not of subjection, I must live so that no one of them may seem to belong to me, and that I may not belong to any of them. It is because I want to be more to them than a friend that I become, to all of them, a stranger.

Therefore, most honorable reader, it is not as an author that I would speak to you, not as a story-teller, not as a philosopher, not as a friend only: I seek to speak to you, in some way, as your own self. Who can tell what this may mean? I myself do not know. But if you listen, things will be said that are perhaps not written in this book. And this will be due not to me, but to One who lives and speaks in both![8]

VI

Preface to the

French Edition

of

THE BLACK

REVOLUTION

December 1963

thomas merton
la révolution noire

Traduit par Marie Tadié

casterman

The Black Revolution *is a bibliographic puzzle and, as a Merton title, may refer to variant items in different languages. Most Merton readers will be familiar with it as the first part of* Seeds of Destruction. The Black Revolution, *as published in France, is in fact this first part of* Seeds of Destruction.

Merton wrote a long essay, "The Black Revolution—Letters to a White Liberal," *in 1963. It was published in the United States in* Ramparts *in December, the same month in which Merton wrote a special preface for the proposed French edition, occasioned in part by the assassination of John F. Kennedy barely a month before. Merton combined this essay with an earlier one, a review of* A Different Drummer *by William M. Kelley, titled in draft* "The Legend of Tucker Caliban," *but called* "The Negro Revolt" *in* Jubilee *in September 1963. Merton changed the title back, combined it with the other essay, and called the tandem piece* "The Black Revolution."

The original essay "The Black Revolution" *was reprinted extensively in entirety and in excerpt in the United States and appeared in periodicals in Chile, Germany and Spain in 1964. The French edition of the "book" with the preface, translated by Marie Tadié, was published in France by Caster-man in mid-1964. In 1965 book-length productions, translated in Cata-lan, Castilian, German, and Italian, and all with the preface, followed.*

In the meantime Merton had been working on a new book for American publication. He called it Cold War and Black Revolution, *combining the two essays on the racial crisis with three essays on peace. He wrote a new preface, called* "Author's Note," *in July 1964 for the whole book, eliminating the preface for the French edition of* The Black Revolution *which was geared toward the first two essays. The publishers, Farrar, Straus and Giroux, had recently brought out a book with the words* "Cold War" *in the title and suggested that Merton change his title to* Seeds of Destruction. *Merton first approved this title,* "an echo of Seeds of Contemplation," *until the Abbot General of the Cistercian Order asked that the essays on peace be deleted. Merton removed two, added new material, and proposed* Seeds of Change *or* Seeds of Revolution *as more appropriate titles. Farrar, Straus preferred their suggestion and the book, with the changes, appeared as* Seeds of Destruction *in November 1964.*

Since The Black Revolution *was published as a separate book in Europe and South America, it might seem that* Seeds of Destruction *would not have been translated in toto from the American edition. But only the French version*, Semences de Destruction, *again translated by Marie Tadié, omitted the first part totally. The Portuguese and Spanish editions were of the entire book, but did not include the preface to the French edition of* The Black Revolution. *The Italian version contained* The Black Revolution *and the preface to the French edition, but a different translator was given credit for both.*

The British edition of Seeds of Destruction *eliminated "The Black Revolution" section. Thomas Burns of Burns and Oates in London wrote to Merton on July 30, 1965, that "the book as it stands would not really do for this side of the Atlantic though practically all of it is valuable over there." And so Merton, who made no objection, dropped "The Black Revolution" part and supplied a new one called "The Church and the Godless World." This altered and different British edition was published in 1966 as* Redeeming the Time, *a title again suggested by the publishers.*

Ironically the eliminated section, considered inappropriate for British publication in 1965, had already been published in Great Britain two years before. It had appeared as "Letters to a White Liberal" in Black-friars, *a periodical from Oxford, beginning in November 1963, one month before American publication in* Ramparts *and before Merton wrote the preface for the French edition.*

This preface, representing Merton's reflections within a month of the event on the assassination of an American president, has thus not been readily available to the English language reader.

Two weeks have not yet elapsed since the assassination of the President of the United States, John Kennedy. A sincere, capable, and above all a reasonable man, acting on Christian principle, he had been trying peacefully to solve the cruel and intricate problem of American racism. Because of the civil rights program which he had initiated and which had earned him the hatred of the South, he had been fiercely attacked in the Southern press, particularly the newspapers of Dallas. Other political figures associated with his liberal program (like Adlai Stevenson and the new President, Lyndon Johnson) had been the target of hostility, even of physical violence in this state, and in this city, not long before Kennedy himself arrived in Dallas.

Yet on the autumn day when he rode through the streets of the Texas city the young President was acclaimed by dense crowds, a fact which shows that the hatred of the South for him was not unanimous. The acclamations made no difference, however, to a man who had taken up his position in a window along the route, a marksman whose rifle, equipped with a telescopic lens, had been purchased from a mail-order house a few months before, evidently with a view to this encounter.

The first thought that everyone had, on hearing the unbelievable news of the President's death, was that he had been shot by Southern racists. Nor was the supposition entirely incongruous, since applause greeted the announcement of his death in some of the Dallas schools. In other areas of the South, citizens refused to fly flags at half-mast. Satisfaction was not always inarticulate nor were all celebrations entirely secret.

It is known, now, that the one who fired the two bullets which struck the President and wounded him fatally was a Southerner, but also an amateur Marxist with a record of shiftlessness and of adventures that may perhaps have been psychopathic. Yet not even the most sanguine of Rightists and super-patriots have managed to argue convincingly that the assassination was the result of a well-laid Communist conspiracy. At the same time, a second fantastic murder, which has silenced the suspected assassin, has shifted the entire problem into a new and uncanny perspective. There is at present no way of saying with certainty what the real motives of the President's assassination were. The crime is under investigation: but will the true solution ever be arrived at? Is it altogether implausible to suppose that there is more in this sinister event than anyone has so far seen? Is it not possible that the assassin was working for someone else, that perhaps many others are involved in his crime? Was the shooting of Oswald in a Dallas police station, under the eyes of the police and of the entire world watching on TV, merely an accident of passion? Yet the American press and public are evidently inclined to accept the sketchy picture of a Leftist malcontent with an itchy trigger-finger, and of a bluff, excitable night club proprietor who "loved all presidents" (we were assured) even to distraction? This is sufficient for the concoction of a mediocre TV script, and few seem to be expecting anything more.

Obviously, this book cannot pretend to solve a crime about which far too little is known, and for which perhaps even the meticulous police investigation may never find the solution. This is not a book about Kennedy, or about his policies, or even about the American South. But it does attempt to understand one aspect of the revolutionary crisis in which the President has met his death. Whatever may be known or said about Lee Oswald the "Marxist" or about Jack Ruby and his rather suspicious connections in the underworld and in the police (for these two sometimes go together nowadays), we must not forget the most obvious fact of all: the President's assassination was simply one in a series of murders which had recently taken place in the South and which were all manifestations of the same confusion, irresponsibility, malice, lawlessness and hatred.

A Baltimore postman, a white man, who had taken upon himself, as a matter of conscience, to walk to Alabama in protest against racism was shot on the roadside shortly after he entered that state. A Negro Leader, an officer of the NAACP, was shot at night when returning to his home at Jackson, Mississippi, after a meeting. Four Negro children died when a bomb exploded in a Baptist Church in Birmingham. On that same Sunday a Negro boy was shot in the street by a white boy who had just come from a racist rally. These last murders occurred barely two months before the shooting of the President. The murderers of the post-man and the Negro Leader are known. The murderer of the Negro boy is known. The question of the bomb in the Baptist Church has been conveniently "forgotten" along with the question of the guilt for scores of other bombings that have taken place in Birmingham and throughout the South. Indeed, even the guilt of those whom everybody knows as murderers has not been punished, since in the South the killing of a Negro by a white man is still not seriously regarded as a crime. There have been loud voices of protest, including at times heroic protest in the South itself: but nothing changes. The sinister current of violence continues on its course. One observation among others has become commonplace: that before the President was killed by the assassin's bullet, he had been assassinated a thousand times and more by Southern tongues and Southern newspapers.

At the root of all this lies a *Schuldfrage*, a question of guilt, that is in every way as momentous as the question of Nazi anti-Semitism. It is a problem of evil and injustice, of hatred and criminal violence, accepted and justified by political and pseudo-ethical slogans. Behind the race hatred which exists both in the North and South, lies a half articulate philosophy of life which one cannot dignify by the name of a "mystique." It is certainly not systematic. It has no rational structure and no clear dogmas like those of Nazism. Yet it is a kind of collective superstition whose roots are all the deeper because they are emotional and unconscious. Thus American racism has something of the character of an ineradicable and axiomatic conviction, which is accepted as the basis for an entire outlook on life and becomes the logical presupposition for inhuman conclusions. The chief of these is the justification of any form of violence, hatred, cruelty, which may be dictated by racist emotions. The justification is sometimes couched in racist terms ("essential inferiority of the Negro"), or sometimes it fits into the more general pattern of anti-communism (since it is also axiomatic that the civil rights movement is "Communistic." Kennedy was openly called a communist throughout the South and this article of faith won massive and unquestioning acceptance).

Hence it appears that a few superficial slogans about freedom and "democracy" are seriously proposed as sufficient reason for any crime, any violation of rights, and anti-communism is called upon to sanctify and consecrate the most outrageous violations of elementary justice.

The phenomenon of racism in the South must, therefore, be accepted in its full reality. But unfortunately this is by no means enough. The guilt that has its roots in the economic history of the Southern United States and which bears these unlovely fruits, is not essentially distinct from the guilt of all those nations which have indulged in colonialistic or expansionistic adventures, whether for profit and capital or for totalitarian power. It is equally related to the racist and the other hatreds which are fomented by Nazism and by Communism. The phenomenon must not be isolated here or there, in Alabama or in South Africa, where it happens to be more evident. It must be seen as worldwide. It is but one aspect of the insecurity, the brutality, the hatred, the stupidity, the frank inhumanity which are so close to the surface of all social life everywhere in the world today. The reasons for this are certainly to some extent economic and sociological. But, if we probe deeper, we find them to be evidence of something much more fundamental: they are symptoms of a world-wide spiritual crisis that may soon reach apocalyptic dimensions, and which has already shown its capacity to do so from time to time, in all societies and in both hemispheres: in Auschwitz, and in Babi-Yar. In Dachau, and also in Norilsk. In Birmingham and Johannesberg, but also in Chicago, Paris, New York, and London. In the bombing of Coventry and Rotterdam, yes: but also in the bombing of Hamburg, Dresden and Berlin. And, as with everything else in our time, all moral roads lead us eventually to Hiroshima and Nagasaki.

The world of the H-bomb is also, inevitably, the world of the dynamite under the stairs of the Third Street Baptist Church. Kennedy himself, a reasonable, peace-loving man, was carrying in his pocket when he was shot a speech he never delivered. It was all about the tremendous growth of weaponry. He was going to speak of all the rockets, all the missiles, all the strategic nuclear weapons, all the tactical weapons too, and all the conventional weapons. He was even going to point out, among other things, that "we have achieved an increase of nearly 600 percent in our special forces that are prepared to work with our allies and friends against guerillas, saboteurs, insurgents and *assassins* . . . " Curious that with all this fantastic weaponry on hand, two bullets from a cheap rifle were all that it took to kill the man who controlled this formidable destructive power!

The assassination of Kennedy is part of the same picture of violence as all the other murders that have taken place everywhere, whether in rioting cities or in the grim silence of prisons, in the name of race, class, or national pride. The picture is that of world-wide hatred, malice, panic, cruelty, destructiveness, a much more dangerous and apocalyptic mood than the fifteenth century dance of death!

Yet we know there are also forces of life, which strive to overcome violence with reason, to meet hatred with love, to accept the inevitable conflicts of political life in a spirit of tolerant understanding and to settle them by peaceful negotiation. These pacific forces are present, and they awaken in protest whenever violence has its way.

But which of these two will prevail? Are we simply to hope that good must, somehow, by its very nature, be victorious? Is the metaphysical analysis of evil as a *non-est* to comfort us with the thought that what is after all "nothing" cannot prevail over the good, which is a transcendental property of being?

Unfortunately, though there may be no "essence" of metaphysical evil, the concrete virulence of its presence makes itself known and felt in things which are indisputably real, and this existential evil must be countered with moral good, or it will prevail over us. But a good that is merely *willed* cannot have power over this evil. Good intentions and fair speeches are not enough. We must begin with the truth. We must know the reality of the good that depends on our decisions and we must also recognize the false good that is incarnate in meaningless slogans or irrational doctrines.

It is strange indeed to see what have been the reactions of various religious groups in America to the evils of racism. Certainly there has been a general attitude of consternation and a wide-spread appeal has been made to the Christian values so often remarkable by their absence from the concrete affairs of life.

In the South, however, large segments of the "Christian" population, not excluding Catholics, have been able with astonishing facility to identify their faith with the recognition of "inequalities willed by God." They have conveniently discovered an ethic which counsels, or even commands, that the Negro be kept under tutelage. In any case their Christianity seems to have little concern with social affairs and is more concentrated on cathartic emotional experiences for the individual. Hence they have felt disappointment with the present trend towards concern with the rights of Negroes. They have manifested indignation over the ministers of the Gospel who, they say, "were all right until they forgot about preaching Jesus and took up this agitation." Such "agitation" is pointed out as yet another piece of evidence that the Churches are "infiltrated with Communists."

At the same time, it is curious indeed to note the sudden outbreak of so-called "charisma" in the South and Mid-west (not to mention the special unspeakable case of Los Angeles). In these areas where even the most distorted conscience cannot help but feel that there is a religious problem that demands to be clarified and solved, where it is evident that truth must be spoken and that Christian and Evangelical principles be shouted from the house-tops as a prelude to serious action, what do we find? Instead of clear preaching and reasonable discussion, we have an outbreak of glossolalia, "speaking with tongues," which is widespread enough to earn the name of a "movement." This supposed "manifestation of the Spirit" is imposing itself not only in the Pentecostal sects which have always been notorious in these matters, but among the Baptists, Methodists and even Episcopalians. What happens, of course, is this: members of the congregation, and also ministers, stand up in turn and give utterance to unintelligible sounds, which they then proceed to "interpret." Comfortingly enough, the interpretation is generally nothing new. And of course it has very little to do with present social realities.

The saner Christian opinion has been slow to mobilize itself, though in the last year the religious press has certainly manifested a keen awareness of the problems, at least outside of the South. Even in the South there have been some explicit and very moving statements, such as that of Bishop Gerow on the murder of Medgar Evers.

It is true also that in many Northern dioceses the Catholic clergy have been preaching on the subject of race. In the South, silence is considered more prudent, and on occasions when this silence is broken (as it was by a friend of mine who is a priest in New Orleans) the racists in the congregation have a tendency to get up and walk out, loudly declaring that they did not come to church to hear "that kind of crap."

There can be no doubt that the death of President Kennedy has done more than a thousand sermons to bring home to the country, and to the world, the critical seriousness of the racial problem. Even though his assassin professed himself a "Marxist" (and there is so far no evidence that official Marxism ever took him seriously), everybody realizes that the assassination was brought about by the powerful and destructive tensions which rend the South and threaten to tear the whole nation in pieces. That is why an instinctive reaction brought all parties together in a temporary show of unity at the President's obsequies. But this has done nothing to assuage the thirst for violence which still remains as real and as dangerous as ever, not only where it has made itself evident, but also where its possibility is not yet actualized.

The present book is therefore an attempt to understand the spiritual pressures that are at work, particularly among the Negroes, in this grave revolutionary crisis. My viewpoint is religious rather than political or sociological. A contemplative monastery is not an appropriate place for the scientific study of social trends. But it does offer the advantage of a unique spiritual perspective. The monk does not, and cannot, simply share the view of the world that is presented in the daily paper which, in any case, he does not consistently read. He is more familiar with the Hebrew prophets than with *Time* and *Life* magazines, but he may also, in exceptional cases, have some access to selected sources of vital information about critical problems in his society. Though he has left "the world" he retains a grave responsibility towards those who have remained in it. This responsibility is spiritual. But in a day when the moral and physical destinies of man are at the mercy of the politician, it is not licit for a so-called "contemplative" wilfully to ignore the major problems of his age.

This book is then a spiritual meditation on a revolutionary crisis: a meditation which, one may hope, has in it an element of Christian truth. In any case, this meditation presupposes that when Churches are bombed and men are shot, the Christian need not resign himself to a choice between silence and—glossolalia!

VII

Preface to the

Japanese Edition

of

SEEDS OF

CONTEMPLATION

March 1965

観想の種子

トマス・マートン著
木鎌安雄訳

In March 1965 Thomas Merton wrote, and wrote quickly, a preface for the Japanese edition of Seeds of Contemplation. *The translator of* Seeds, *Yasuwo Kikama, wrote to Merton toward the end of February informing him that he had completed his translation and requesting that Merton write a special preface for this edition, a preface calculated to introduce the work to Japanese readers. Merton responded on March 10 that he would be "delighted" to write the preface, that he hoped it would be a "worthwhile preface rather than just a few banal phrases." Merton's interest in Japan and in doing such a special preface was so great at this point that he wrote, revised, and corrected the preface in less than a week and the completed version was in Kikama's hands in Japan by March 25.*

Kikama's translation, called Kansō no Shushi, *was the first Japanese effort with which Merton had been more or less directly involved. Despite his involvement and his earlier permission to Kikama to translate* Seeds, *a misunderstanding, largely prompted by Merton's chronic vagueness about foreign rights, developed and a second Japanese edition without a special preface, translated by Junji Nagasawa and called* Meisō no Shushi, *appeared in 1966. Oddly neither used Merton's revision of the book,* New Seeds of Contemplation, *published in 1961, which had superseded* Seeds *in the United States, but instead translated from the older 1949 edition.*

This was actually the second preface for a Japanese edition that Merton wrote. As already noted, he had done one for the translation of The Seven Storey Mountain *in 1963, but production problems delayed publication until 1966. The preface for* Seeds of Contemplation *came out first and thus contained Merton's initial statement directed to Japanese readers.*

The text has been edited and compiled from two sources, Merton's original typescript with his holographic revisions, corrections, and additions and his mimeograph version, both completed in March 1965. No material which Merton had marked out or deleted has been included, but two passages, bracketed in this version which appear in the typescript but not in the mimeograph version through obvious typographical error, have been included. Merton reworked this preface, added a modicum of new material, and it was published in India in the fall of 1965 under the title "The Contemplative Life in the Modern World" in The Mountain Path, *organ of the followers of Sri Ramana Maharsi. He later included it with this title in the 1968 collection* Faith and Violence.

Can contemplation still find a place in the world of technology and conflict which is ours? Does it belong only to the past? The answer to this is that, since the direct and pure experience of reality in its ultimate root is man's deepest need, contemplation must be possible if man is to remain human. If contemplation is no longer possible, then man's life has lost the spiritual orientation upon which everything else—order, peace, happiness, sanity—must depend. But true contemplation is an austere and exacting vocation. Those who seek it are few and those who find it fewer still. Nevertheless, their presence [bears] witness to the fact that contemplation remains both necessary and possible.

When this book was first published in the United States, in 1949, it was read rather eagerly by many who perhaps sought in it not the reality of contemplation but a dream, an evasion, a tempting and illusory realm of peace that could be achieved by withdrawal.

Man has an instinctive need for harmony and peace, for tranquility, order and meaning. None of those seem to be the most salient characteristics of modern society. A book written in a monastery where the traditions and rites of a more contemplative age are still alive and still practised, could not help but remind men that there had once existed a more leisurely and more spiritual way of life—and that this was the way of their ancestors. Thus even into the confused pattern of Western life is woven a certain memory of contemplation. It is a memory so vague and so remote that it is hardly understood, and yet it can awaken the hope of recovering inner peace. In this hope, modern man can perhaps entertain, for a brief time, the dream of a contemplative life and of a higher spiritual state of quiet, of rest, of untroubled joy. But a sense of self-deception and guilt immediately awakens a reaction of despair, disgust, a rejection of the dream and a commitment to total activism. We must face the fact that the mere thought of contemplation is one which deeply troubles the person who takes it seriously. It is so contrary to the modern way of life, so apparently alien, so seemingly impossible, that the modern man who even considers it finds, at first, that his whole being rebels against it. If the ideal of inner peace remains attractive, the demands of the way to peace seem to be so exacting and so extreme that they can no longer be met. We would like to be quiet, but our restlessness will not allow it. Hence we believe that for us there can be no peace except in a life filled up with movement and activity, with speech, news, communication, recreation, distraction. We seek the meaning of our life in activity for its own sake, activity without objective, efficacy without fruit, scientism, the cult of unlimited power, the service of the machine as an end in itself. And in all these a certain dynamism is imagined. The life of frantic activity is invested with the noblest of qualities, as if it were the whole end and happiness of man: or rather as if the life of man had no inherent meaning whatever and that it had to be given a meaning from some external source, from a society engaged in a gigantic communal effort to raise man above himself. Man is indeed called to transcend himself. But do his own efforts suffice for this?

The reason for this inner confusion and conflict is that our technological society has no longer any place in it for wisdom that seeks truth for its own sake, that seeks the fulness of being, that seeks to rest in an intuition of the very ground of all being. Without wisdom, the apparent opposition of action and contemplation, of work and rest, of involvement and detachment, can never be resolved. Ancient and traditional societies, whether of Asia or of the West, always specifically recognized "the way" of the wise, the way of spiritual discipline in which there was at once wisdom and method, and by which, whether in art, in philosophy, in religion, or in the monastic life, some men would attain to the inner meaning of being, they would *experience* this meaning for all their brothers, they would so to speak bring together in themselves the divisions or complications that confused the life of their fellows. By healing the divisions in themselves they would help heal the divisions of the whole world. They would realize in themselves that unity which is at the same time the highest action and the purest rest, true knowledge and self-less love, a knowledge beyond knowledge in emptiness and unknowing; a willing beyond will in apparent non-activity. They would attain to the highest striving in the absence of striving and of contention.

This way of wisdom is no dream, no temptation and no evasion, for it is on the contrary a return to reality in its very root. It is not an escape from contradiction and confusion for it finds unity and clarity only by plunging into the very midst of contradiction, by the acceptance of emptiness and suffering, by the renunciation of the passions and obsessions with which the whole world is "on fire". It does not withdraw from the fire. It is in the very heart of the fire, yet remains cool, because it has the gentleness and humility that come from self-abandonment, and hence does not seek to assert the illusion of the exterior self.

Of course, it must be admitted that this book was written in a monastery. And the author remains in the same monastery nearly twenty years later, still convinced of the reality of the way he seeks to travel, still seeking to understand better the illusions that are met with in this way but not in order to abandon the way. Once a man has set his foot on this way, there is no excuse for abandoning it, for to be actually on the way is to recognize without doubt or hesitation that only the way is fully real and that everything else is deception, except in so far as it may in some secret and hidden manner be connected with "the way".

Thus, far from wishing to abandon this way, the author seeks only to travel further and further along it. This journey without maps leads him into rugged mountainous country where there are often mists and storms and where he is more and more alone. Yet at the same time, ascending the slopes in darkness, feeling more and more keenly his own emptiness, and with the winter wind blowing cruelly through his now tattered garments, he meets at times other travellers on the way, poor pilgrim as he is, and as solitary as he, belonging perhaps to other lands and other traditions. There are of course great differences between them, and yet they have much in common. Indeed, the author of this book can say that he feels himself much closer to the Zen monks of ancient Japan than to the busy and impatient men of the West, of his own country, who think in terms of money, power, publicity, machines, business, political advantage, military strategy—who seek, in a word, the triumphant affirmation of their own will, their own power, considered as the end for which they exist. Is not this perhaps the most foolish of all dreams, the most tenacious and damaging of illusions?

In any event, it is certain that the way of wisdom is not an evasion. Simply to evade modern life would be a futile attempt to abdicate from its responsibilities [while clinging to its advantages. The way of contemplation is a way of higher and more permanent responsibilities] and a renunciation of advantages—and illusions. The contemplative way requires first of all and above all renunciation of this obsession with the triumph of the individual or collective will to power. For this aggressive and self-assertive drive to possess and to exert power implies a totally different view of reality than that which is seen when one travels the contemplative way. The aggressive and dominative view of reality places, at the center, the individual self with its bodily form, its feelings and emotions, its appetites and needs, its loves and hates, its actions and reactions. All these are seen as forming together a basic and indubitable reality to which everything else must be referred, so that all other things are also estimated in their individuality, their actions and reactions, and all the ways in which they impinge upon the interests of the individual self. The world is then seen as a multiplicity of conflicting and limited beings, all enclosed in the limits of their own individuality, all therefore complete in a permanent and vulnerable incompleteness, all seeking to find a certain completeness by asserting themselves at the expense of others, dominating and using others. This world becomes, then, an immense conflict in which the only peace is that which is accorded to the victory of the strong, and in order to taste the joy of this peace, the weak must submit to the strong and join him in his adventures so that they may share in his power. Thus there arises a spurious, inconclusive unity: the unity of the great aggregate, the unity of those thrown together without love and without understanding by the accidents of the power struggle. Seen from the point of view of "the way" this unity is nothing but a collective monstrosity because it has no real reason for existing and is not a unity at all. However insistently it may claim for itself the dignities of a truly communal and human existence, it does not elevate man by a truly communal and interpersonal cooperation. It only drives him with mad and irresistible demands, exploiting him, alienating him from reality and demanding from him a blind irrational and total subjection. The life of the collective mass is such that it destroys in man the inmost need and capacity for contemplation. It dries up the living springs of compassion and understanding. It perverts the creative genius and destroys the innocent vision that is proper to man in communion with nature. Finally the collective mass becomes a vast aggregate of organized hatred, a huge and organized death-wish, threatening its own existence and that of the entire human race.

The mission of the contemplative in this world of massive conflict and collective unreason is to seek the true way of unity and peace, without succumbing to the illusion of withdrawal into a realm of abstraction from which unpleasant realities are simply excluded by the force of will. In facing the world with a totally different viewpoint, he maintains alive in the world the presence of a spiritual and intelligent consciousness which is the root of true peace and true unity among men. This consciousness certainly accepts the fact of our empirical and individual existence, but refuses to take this as the basic reality. The basic reality is neither the individual, empirical self nor an abstract and ideal entity which can exist only in reason. The basic reality is being itself, which is one in all concrete existents, which shares itself among them and manifests itself through them. The goal of the contemplative is, on its lowest level, the recognition of this splendor of being and unity—a splendor in which he is one with all that is. But on a higher level still, it is the transcendent ground and source of being, the not-being and the emptiness that is so called because it is absolutely beyond all definitions and limitation. This ground and source is not simply an inert and passive emptiness, but for the Christian it is pure act, pure freedom, pure light. The emptiness which is "pure being" is the light of God which, as St. John's Gospel says, "gives light to every man who comes into the world." Specifically, the Gospel sees all being coming forth from the Father, God, in His Word, who is the light of the world. "In Him (the Word) was life, and this life was Light for all men, and the Light shone in darkness and the darkness could not understand it." (John 1: 4-5)

Now very often the ordinary active and ethical preoccupations of Christians make them forget this deeper and more contemplative dimension of the Christian way. So active, in fact, has been the face presented by Christianity to the Asian world that the hidden contemplative element of Christianity is often not even suspected at all by Asians. But without the deep root of wisdom and contemplation, Christian action would have no meaning and no purpose.

The Christian is then not simply a man of good will, who commits himself to a certain set of beliefs, who has a definite dogmatic conception of the universe, of man, and of man's reason for existing. He is not simply one who follows a moral code of brotherhood and benevolence with strong emphasis on certain rewards and punishments dealt out to the individual. Underlying Christianity is not simply a set of doctrines about God considered as dwelling remotely in heaven, and man struggling on earth, far from heaven, trying to appease a distant God by means of virtuous acts. On the contrary Christians themselves too often fail to realize that the infinite God is dwelling within them, so that He is in them and they are in Him. They remain unaware of the presence of the infinite source of being right in the midst of the world and of men. True Christian wisdom is therefore oriented to the experience of divine Light which is present in the world, the Light in whom all things are, and which is nevertheless unknown to the world because no mind can see or grasp its infinity. "He was in the world and the world was made by Him and the world did not know Him. He came into His own and His own did not receive Him." (John 1: 10-11)

Contemplative wisdom is then not simply an aesthetic extrapolation of certain intellectual or dogmatic principles, but a living contact with the Infinite Source of all being, a contact not only of minds and hearts, not only of "I and Thou", but a transcendent union of consciousness in which man and God become, according to the expression of St. Paul "one spirit".

Though this contemplative union is an extreme intensification of conscious awareness, a kind of *total awareness*, it is not properly contained or signified in any particular vision, but rather in non-vision which attains the totality of meaning beyond all limited conceptions, by the surrender of love. God Himself is not only pure being but also pure love, and to know Him is to become one with Him in love. In this dimension of Christian experience, the Cross of Christ means more than the juridical redemption of man from the guilt of evil-doing. It means the passage from death to life and from nothingness to fullness, or to fullness in nothingness. Thus the contemplative way of ancient Christian monastic tradition is not simply a way of emptiness and transcendence in union with the crucified Christ. The Cross signifies that the sacrificial death which is indeed the destruction of the empirical bodily existence and end of all lust for earthly power and all indulgence of passion, is in fact the liberation of those who have renounced this exterior self in order to dedicate their lives to love and to truth. Christ is not simply an object of love and contemplation whom the Christian considers with devout attention: He is also "the way, the truth and the life" so that for the Christian to be "on the way" is to be "in Christ" and to seek truth is to walk in the light of Christ. "For me to live," says St. Paul, "is Christ. I live, now not I, but Christ lives in me."

This is a summary outline of the meaning of Christian contemplation, a meaning which calls for much greater development particularly in all that concerns the sacramental and liturgical life of the Church.

Such is the way of contemplation that is the subject of this book. But the book is not a systematic treatise. It is only a collection of intuitions and hints, which seek rather to suggest than to define. Nowhere do they claim to present a systematic philosophy or theology, still less an apologetic for Christian ideas.

To read this book one does not need to be a Christian: it is sufficient that one is a man, and that he has in himself the instinct for truth, the desire of that freedom from limitation and from servitude to external things which St. Paul calls the "servitude of corruption" and which, in fact, holds the whole world of man in bondage by passion, greed, the lust for sensation and for individual survival, as though one could become rich enough, powerful enough and clever enough to cheat death.

Unfortunately, this passion for unreality and for the impossible fills the world today with violence, hatred, and indeed with a kind of insane and cunning fury which threatens our very existence.

Science and technology are indeed admirable in many respects and if they fulfill their promises they can do much for man. But they can never solve his deepest problems. On the contrary without wisdom, without the intuition and freedom that enable man to return to the root of his being, science can only precipitate him still further into the centrifugal flight that flings him, in all his compact and uncomprehending isolation, into the darkness of outer space without purpose and without objective.

NOTE:

The Abbey of Gethsemani, where this book was written, is a community of contemplative monks of the Cistercian Order (Trappists), famous for its dedication to silence, manual labor, solitude, meditation and liturgical worship. The Abbey was founded in Kentucky, one of the Southern States of the U.S., in 1848 by monks from France. The monks observe the Rule of St. Benedict in its strict interpretation and do not engage in teaching or in preaching, though in some exceptional cases they write books. There is one monastery of the same Order in Japan, as well as several convents of nuns.

VIII

Preface to the

Korean Edition

of

LIFE AND

HOLINESS

July 1965

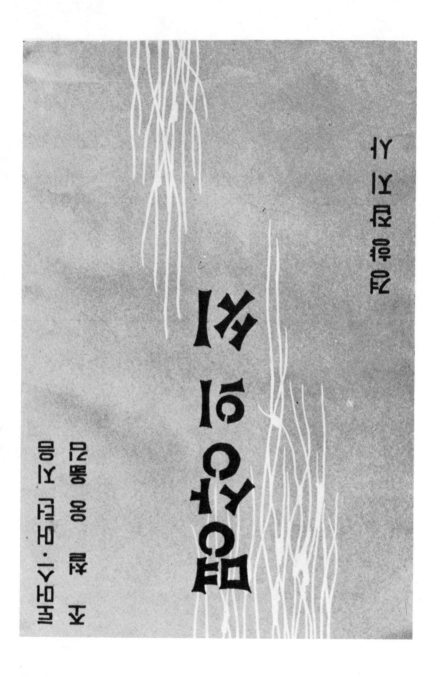

In late 1964 Thomas Merton wrote to Rev. Paul Jeong-jim Kim of the Holy Ghost Monastery in Seoul, South Korea, who proposed to translate Life and Holiness *into Korean. He told Fr. Kim that he gave his approbation for a translation and that he would be glad to supply "a brief foreword" for the Korean edition once Kim received a "green light" from the American publishers, Herder and Herder, to proceed. Kim received the green light and Merton wrote a preface, the only one he did for a Korean translation, in July 1965. Similar to his preface for the Japanese edition of* Seeds of Contemplation, *it was an attempt to show Korean readers that Western Christianity had a contemplative as well as an active side. At least one other major Merton work,* Seeds of Contemplation *without a special preface, had been published in South Korea and Merton had sent articles to friends for translation and inclusion in* The Catholic Times, *a weekly publication in Seoul.*

Life and Holiness, *published in the United States in 1963, was one of Merton's more successful books although he rated it only "Fair" and preferred most of his other writings to it. But the American paperback edition (1964) has remained consistently in print and it has been translated, besides into Korean, into Catalan, Castilian, French, German, Hungarian, Italian, Japanese, Netherlandic, Portuguese, and Slovene. The Korean edition was published in Seoul in 1965 with the title* Hyeondaeineui Sinang Saenghwal. *Merton did only one special preface for this popular book, this for the Korean edition, seeing it as a chance, as he says, "to express his deep love for his brothers and sisters in Korea." He never reworked the preface and it has not previously been published in English.*

The fact that Christianity developed in the West, and that Christendom or "Christian culture" has been for so long identifiable with European culture, makes us forget that Christianity is, from the European viewpoint, originally "oriental." The cultural features which Christianity acquired from its acclimatization in Europe are not all necessarily Christian. Hence, Christianity sometimes presents the aspect of an intensely active, individualistic, ethical system, based on a body of dogmatic truths which tend to define God objectively and to give a clear, definitive explanation of His will and of His plans for the world. What remains for man is then to accept these various speculative descriptions and explanations, and to live an energetic, progressive, productive life full of uprightness and good works.

This active concept of Christianity seems to imply that to be "Christian" means also to be "modern," "progressive," and "western." For those who favor Western ideas, this view of Christianity may prove attractive. But Christianity is not identified with any particular culture. It is indeed a religion that looks to the future, but it does not place its hopes merely in human progress. The hope of the Christian is indeed a hope for man, but it places its confidence in God, and not in man.

The hidden God, of whose being we are obscurely conscious when we are conscious of our own life and freedom, but whom we cannot see, adequately define or clearly explain, has indeed revealed Himself. But He has not really manifested in clear light the inner mystery of His hidden nature as He is in Himself. What He has revealed in the Gospel is His *love for man*. This love has opened to us a way of salvation, in which we hear His voice calling us to a fulfillment which we do not at first understand, but which can be attained if we obey His mysterious will. This will is something more than an external law. It is a life in which God Himself lives in us, by His Holy Spirit.

Christianity is first of all a way of life, rather than a way of thought. Merely to study Christian truths and gain intellectual understanding of them is not enough. Indeed, study does not, by itself, bring us to a complete understanding of them. It is only by living the Christian life that we come to understand the full meaning of the Christian message. The meaning of this message is precisely that God has come to dwell in man and to show, in man, that the sorrows, sufferings and defeats inherent in human existence can never deprive man's life of meaning as long as he is capable of deciding to live as a son of God and consents to let God live and triumph in his own heart. This is not merely a matter of individual consolation, but of fraternal love. The Christian bears witness to God's love for the world by living a communal life in which the presence of Christ is obscurely manifest in the love of brethren for one another.

One cannot live the Christian life as it is meant to be lived without seeking to be holy. In order to be holy one must become free from the tyranny and the demands of sin, of lust, of anger, of pride, ambition, injustice and the spirit of violence. When one sincerely renounces sin and selfish living, one begins to find something of the peace and serenity which come from the awareness that God lives and acts in us. However, the "old man" of sin is not yet dead in us. Soon there begins a new phase of struggle and uncertainty, in which we learn that holiness is not easy, and is not just a matter of will power and good intentions. In this difficult struggle we gain experience of our own limitations and weakness. But we also learn, by experience, that if we trust in the power of God, and seek to imitate His Beloved Son, Jesus Christ, in His passion and His victory, we receive mysterious strength that has no human source. Then we begin to become more closely identified with Christ and to realize, at least in the silence of the heart that loves and trusts Him, that He Himself lives in us and is our strength. Jesus Christ is our new and hidden self. Our true way of life is then to renounce our old external self, with its selfish desires and its illusions, in order that Christ may fully live in us. It is thus that we begin to be truly Christians. For then the new life that began in us sacramentally by baptism becomes a matter of everyday experience, since Christ takes possession of our being in order that He Himself may be life, holiness and wisdom in us.

The Christian way necessarily begins with learning how to obey certain standards of conduct, but it soon becomes a way of simple obedience to God in the Spirit of love which dwells in His

Church, the assembly of all the faithful who are One in Christ. This communal aspect of Christian holiness is important. Christian perfection is not merely the stern ascetic detachment of the individual who has set himself to follow a heroic way of renunciation. It is above all a communion in the joyous love of Christ living in His Church. It is a sharing in the joy of faith, a participation in worship and in spiritual light, a common life in the Holy Spirit. From this life no one is excluded—not the poor, not the despised, not the unfortunate sinner who consents to be loved and to return to Christ.

To be a Christian is then not only to believe in Christ, but to live as Christ and, in a mysterious way, to become united with Christ. This is both Christian life and Christian holiness.

The way of Christian holiness is then not a way of extraordinary virtue and of miraculous powers, but of simple fidelity and love in the ordinary life of every day. The work, the family life, the simple consolations and the ordinary sufferings of Christians are lived in a new Spirit, and filled with the love and faith that seek only God's will, not personal profit and gratification.

This book is written for Christians who have decided they cannot be content with a merely external practice of their religion. They are not content with merely "fulfilling their obligations" and living lives that are "correct." They realize that one can be outwardly good without interiorly knowing Christ, but they are not satisfied with a life that does not know Him. They believe that their Christian vocation means an interior revolution in which what seems to be their "self" is gradually destroyed and exchanged for another deeper self, the Spirit of Christ. Such Christians are true Christians who know that "God is love" and who seek nothing but to abandon themselves to this love. It is in loving God that they learn to love other men as themselves. By their love, they manifest that God dwells among men.

But to live this life of love today requires great courage and patience. The world is in crisis. A kind of madness sweeps through human society, threatening to destroy it altogether. The faith, the love and the patience of saints are the only forces that can save us from this destruction. The Christian, in deep compassion, must seek to help his fellow man to escape from the terrible effects of greed and hatred. He must therefore be concerned with social justice and with peace on earth. It would be a grave mistake to confuse Christianity with the ideology of power and force which sometimes influences the policies of certain nations that appeal to Christianity to justify themselves.

It is clear that Asian and African Christians must learn more and more to create certain authentic forms of Christian witness that are clearly their own, and are not dominated by cultural ideas and prejudices borrowed from the western world.

This translation enables the author to express his deep love for his brothers and sisters in Korea and to assure them of his prayers, while asking that they pray for him that he may be faithful in the task appointed to him in the Church.

IX

Preface to the

Spanish Edition

of

SEEDS OF

DESTRUCTION

A   Christmas   Letter

1965

December 1965

Thomas Merton

SEMILLAS
DE
DESTRUC-
CION

ENSAYOS CONTEMPORÁNEOS

The preface to the Spanish edition of Seeds of Destruction *was not conceived nor written as a special preface to a foreign edition. At Christmas 1965 Merton, because of the crush of correspondence and his inability to respond to it adequately, began sending occasional mimeographed letters to his friends. These letters demonstrate beautifully his style as a letter writer, a style incorporating information, informality, chattiness, and honesty. He wrote the 1965 letter for a particular purpose. In it he notified his friends of his retirement to the hermitage, his seeking a greater solitude, and his intention to write and comment less on current events and issues.*

It was this last declaration which prompted José Maria Valverde, long-time friend and correspondent of Merton's and a recipient of the Christmas letter, to ask Merton if he might include it as a special preface to his translation of Seeds of Destruction. *Since that work represented so well Merton's concern with contemporary events, Valverde thought it would be appropriate to inform Spanish readers of his intended withdrawal from speaking so frequently and so openly on such topics. Merton approved the project and the letter was printed in* Semillas de Destrucción, *published by Pomaire in Barcelona in 1966, as "A Modo de Prólogo de la Traducción Española."*

Merton's intention of maintaining a greater aloofness from events of his time never developed. In the three remaining years of his life, after he wrote the Christmas 1965 letter, he continued to speak from his hermitage on problems of peace, of war, of human rights and social justice. But that does not alter the sincerity of this letter nor the good faith with which Valverde offered it to Spanish readers. The letter, circulated widely in mimeograph form, has not been published in English.

A CHRISTMAS LETTER   1965
ABBEY OF GETHSEMANI, KY.

Dear Friend:

I hate to resort to mimeographed letters but it has become completely impossible for me to answer most of my mail personally. Last summer I received permission to do something I had been hoping for since my early days in the monastery. I am living in solitude and trying to do the things that I really came here for. This means that to a great extent I have to sacrifice the semi-public life of the writer, though I will continue to do some writing. Correspondence has been greatly reduced. Anyway it is pretty cold now where I am and this means I have to keep busy cutting wood besides other work.

Visits have practically been suspended and I am in no position to conduct spiritual direction by mail. Also I receive dozens of books, brochures, poems, manuscripts and others things which are sent to me. I cannot comment on them all.*

The monastic life by its nature should open out into a greater solitude with more attention given to prayer, meditation, study, and the real business of the monk which is to seek God alone. I realize that this is not something that everyone agrees with, but for some people this is a real necessity since they are called to it by God. Hence I ask your prayers that I may be able to do what He asks of me and be faithful to my vocation.

As a result of this more solitary life I am not involved in any kind of direct political action. It is true that I am still convinced, together with Pope Paul and the Council, that the Church must help man to work for the abolition of war and to overcome all the other evils which confront us. I am certainly concerned about this as a pastoral issue and do not intend to remain entirely silent on it, in this sense. But I do not see where I can do any good by engaging in political controversy when I am not in a position to keep up with events and judge them objectively.

---

*This paragraph does not appear in the original draft of the Christmas Letter. It is, however, included in translation in the Spanish Edition.

Be sure that I appreciate your letters. I am always glad to get news of my friends and I keep you all in my prayers. I will remember you at Mass and doubtless often during the day. I hope you are well and happy and pray for you to be so. I wish you all the joys of Christmas and a happy New Year. May God give you a deeper faith, more light, more strength and grace to accept and follow His will with greater peace and clarity. May you have greater trust in Him and may He bring us all to rejoice together in His light. God bless you.

Cordially yours in Christ,

Thomas Merton

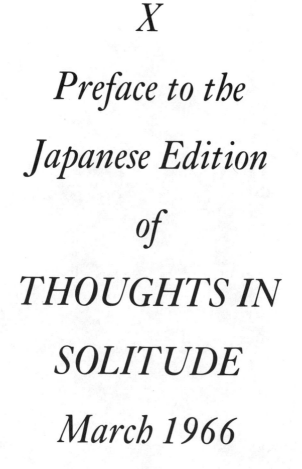

X

Preface to the

Japanese Edition

of

THOUGHTS IN

SOLITUDE

March 1966

孤独の中の思索

トマス・マートン 著

木鎌安雄訳

THOUGHT IN SOLITUDE
by Thomas Merton

新装版

Thoughts in Solitude, *Thomas Merton's book of musings, a collection lacking the apparent coherence and tightness of some of his productions, which he originally called simply* Thirty-seven Meditations, *has emerged as one of his more popular and enduring works. Published by Farrar, Straus and Cudahy in 1958, it has gone through three subsequent American editions, two British editions, and translation into Chinese, German, Italian, Japanese, Polish, Portuguese, and Spanish. It was one of the thirteen books which Merton rated "Better" on his graph evaluating his own work. He gave the "Best" rating to no book at all, indicating that he perhaps felt he had not produced his masterwork.*

He wrote a second preface for his friend and translator, Yasuwo Kikama, for the Japanese edition of Thoughts *in March 1966. With one special preface already published and another imminent, he felt no need to introduce himself or to explain Western tradition to Japanese readers. Instead he wrote a preface similar to those he wrote for the books of other writers, a preface compatible with the book but one which expands and extends the book rather than merely introducing it. The preface is not a preface in the usual sense. Merton mentioned the book that would follow, but the book is really incidental, though complementary, to the thrust of the preface. The preface is itself an essay on solitude, a meditation as the body of the book is a series of meditations. It sets a mood for what follows, but it could be removed from the book without damage to the book or to the essay.*

Merton wrote the first draft in March, significantly revised and added to it, and had copies mimeographed for distribution in April. He sent this mimeographed version to Kikama for inclusion in the Japanese edition. After sending that version to Japan, Merton again revised and enlarged the essay. One mimeograph copy has Merton's notation "more complete version in the Critic." The Critic *printed this fuller version, titled "Love and Solitude," in November 1966.*

The version included here is the middle one, the one sent to Kikama in mimeograph and the one translated into Japanese. The first draft, Merton's thoughts as he originally set them down before he revised and reworked in his usual way is included as an appendix to show something of Merton's style as a writer. The last and "more complete" version may be consulted in The Critic. *The Japanese edition,* Kodoku no naka no Shisaku, *was published, printed in Japanese, by Veritas Publishing Company in Tokyo in late 1966. Unlike most of the other prefaces, it appeared, as "Love and Solitude," in the United States at the same time and was thus available to English-language readers. It has since been included in the collection,* Love and Living, *edited by Brother Patrick Hart and published in 1979.*

No writing on the solitary, meditative dimensions of life can say anything that has not already been said better by the wind in the pine trees. These pages seek nothing more than to echo the silence and peace that is "heard" when the rain wanders freely among the hills and forests. But what can the wind say where there is no hearer? There is then a deeper silence: the silence in which the Hearer is No-Hearer. That deeper silence must be heard before one can speak truly of solitude.

These pages do not attempt to convey any special information, or to answer deep philosophical questions about life. True, they do concern themselves with questions about life. But they certainly do not pretend to do the reader's thinking for him. On the contrary, they invite him to listen for himself. They do not merely speak to him, they remind him that he is a Hearer.

But who is this Hearer?

Beyond the Hearer, is there perhaps No-Hearer?

Who is this No-Hearer?

For such outrageous questions there are no intelligible answers. The only answer is the Hearing itself. The proper climate for such Hearing is solitude.

Or perhaps better, this Hearing which is No-Hearing is itself solitude. Why do I speak of a Hearing which is No-Hearing? Because if you imagine the solitary as "one" who has numerically isolated himself from "many others," who has simply gone out of the crowd to hang up his individual number on a rock in the desert, and there to receive messages denied to the many, you have a false and demonic solitude. This is solipsism, not solitude. It is the false unity of separateness, in which the individual marks himself off as his own number, affirms himself by saying "count me out."

The true unity of the solitary life is the one in which there is no possible division. The true solitary does not seek himself, but loses himself. He forgets that there is number, in order to become all. Therefore he is No (individual) Hearer.

He is attuned to all the Hearing in the world, since he lives in silence. He does not listen to the ground of being, but he identifies himself with that ground in which all being hears and knows itself.

Therefore he no longer has a thought for himself. What is this ground, this unity? It is Love. The paradox of solitude is that its true ground is universal love—and true solitude is the undivided unity of love for which there is no number.

The world is shrinking. There is less and less space in which men can be alone. It is said that if we go on increasing at our present rate, then in six hundred and fifty years there will be only one square foot left for every person. Even then, (someone may say) there will be one square foot of solitude. But is that right? Is each person a separate solitude of his own? No. There is One Solitude in which all persons are at once together and alone. But the price of a mathematical, quantitative concept of man (for instance in a positivistic and sociological approach) is that in reducing each individual to his own number it reduces him to nothing; and in making the mass of men simply a total of individual units, it makes of it an enormous statistical void—a void in which numbers simply proliferate without aim, without value, without meaning, without love.

The peril of this massive, numerical, technical concept of man, then, is that it destroys love by substituting the individual for the person. And what is the person? Precisely he is one in the unity which is love. He is undivided in himself because he is open to all. He is open to all because the one love that is the source of all, the form of all and the end of all, is one in him and in all. He is truly alone who is wide open to heaven and earth and closed to no one.

Love is not a problem, not an answer to a question. Love knows no question. It is the ground of all, and questions arise only insofar as we are divided, absent, estranged, alienated from that ground.

But the precise nature of our society is to bring about this division, this alienation, this estrangement, this absence. Hence we live in a world in which, though we clutter it with out possessions, our projects, our exploitations and our machinery, we ourselves are absent. Hence we live in a world in which we say "God is dead," and do so in a sense rightly, since we are no longer capable of experiencing the truth that we are completely rooted and grounded in His Love.

How can we rediscover this Truth?

Only when we no longer need to seek it—for as long as we seek it we imply that we have lost it. But in fact, to recognize ourselves as grounded in our true ground, love, is to recognize that we cannot be without it.

This recognition is impossible without a basic personal solitude.

Collective agitation, no matter how much it expostulates about "I and Thou" will never attain it. For in the ground of solitude, "I and Thou" are one. And only from this ground does true dilection grow. Let us not then make "love" and "solitude" a matter of question and answer. The answer is not found in words, but by living on a certain level of consciousness. These pages are, then, concerned with a spiritual climate, an atmosphere, a landscape of the mind, a level of consciousness: the peace, the silence of aloneness in which the Hearer listens, and the Hearing is No-Hearing.

Christianity is a religion of the Word. The Word is Love. But we sometimes forget that the Word emerges first of all from silence. When there is no silence, then the One Word which God speaks is not truly heard as Love. Then only "words" are heard. "Words" are not love, for they are many and Love is One. Where there are many words, we lose consciousness of the fact that there is really only One Word. The One Word which God speaks is Himself. Speaking, he manifests Himself as infinite Love. His speaking and His hearing are One. So silent is His speech that, to our way of thinking, His speech is no speech, His hearing is no-hearing. Yet in His silence, in the abyss of His one Love, all words are spoken and all words are heard. Only in this silence of infinite Love do they have coherence and meaning. Yet we draw them out of silence in order to separate them from one another, to make them distinct, to give them a unique sound by which we can discern them. This is necessary. Yet in all these many sounds and concepts there remains the hidden, secret power of one silence, one love, which is the power of God. "When all things were enveloped in quiet silence," says the Book of Wisdom (18:14), "and when the night had reached the mid-point in its course, from the height of the heavens, Thy all powerful Word leaped down from the royal throne."[1] By the action that takes place in life and history, the secret nonaction of Word and power manifest their reality. In this deep silence, Love remains the ground of history.

Even though one may be a learned man and may have profound knowledge of many subjects, and many "words," this is of no value; it has no central meaning, if the One Word, Love, has not been heard. That One Word is heard only in the silence and solitude of the empty heart, the selfless, undivided heart, the heart that is at peace, detached, free, without care. In the language of Christianity, this freedom is the realm of faith, and hope, but above all of Love. "If I have perfect faith . . . but no Love, I am nothing" (I Cor. 13:2). "Anyone who does not Love is still in death" (I John 3:14).

When the Christian faith is made to appear very complicated, it seems to consist of numerous doctrines, a complex system of concepts which impart information about the supernatural and seems to answer all possible questions about the afterlife, and about the means to attain to happiness in heaven. While these doctrines may be very true, they cannot be understood if we think that the only purpose of faith is multiple information communicated in many complex doctrines. In fact, the object of faith is One—God, Love. And though the revealed doctrines about Him are true, yet what they tell us of Him is not fully adequate as long as we grasp them only separately, incoherently, without living unity in Love. They must converge upon Love as the spokes of a wheel converge upon a central hub. They are window frames through which the One Light enters our houses. The window frame is precise and distinct; yet what we really see is the light itself which is diffuse and all-pervading so that it is everywhere and nowhere. No mind can comprehend God's reality as it is in itself, and if we approach Him we must advance not only by knowing but by not-knowing. We must seek to communicate with Him not only by words but above all by silence in which there is only the One Word, and the One Word is infinite Love and endless silence.

Where is silence? Where is solitude? Where is Love? Ultimately, these cannot be found anywhere except in the ground of our own being. There, in the silent depths, there is no more distinction between the I and the Not-I. There is perfect peace because we are grounded in infinite creative and redemptive Love. There we encounter God, whom no eye can see, and in Whom, as St. Paul says, "we live and move and have our being" (Acts 17:28). In Him, too, we find solitude, as St. John of the Cross said, we find that the All and the Nothing encounter one another and are the Same.

If there is no silence beyond and within the many words of doctrine, there is no religion, only a religious ideology. For religion goes beyond words and actions, and attains to the ultimate truth only in silence and Love. Where this silence is lacking, where there are only the "many words" and not the One Word, then there is much bustle and activity, but no peace, no deep thought, no understanding, no inner quiet. Where there is no peace, there is no light and no Love. The mind that is hyperactive seems to itself to be awake and productive, but it is dreaming, driven by fantasy and doubt. One must know how to return to the quiet of worship, the reverent peace of prayer, the adoration in which the entire ego-self silences and abases itself in the presence of the Invisible God to receive His one Word of Love. In these "activities" which are "nonactions" the spirit truly wakes from the dream of a multifarious, confused and agitated existence. Rooted in non-action, we are ready to act in everything.

Precisely because of this lack, modern Western man is afraid of solitude. He is unable to be alone, to be silent. He is communicating his spiritual and mental sickness to men of the East. Asia is gravely tempted by the violence and activism of the West and is gradually losing hold of its traditional respect for silent wisdom. Therefore it is all the more necessary at this time to rediscover the climate of solitude and of silence; not that everyone can go apart and live alone. But in moments of silence, of meditation, of enlightenment and peace, one learns to be silent and alone everywhere. One learns to lie in the atmosphere of solitude even in the midst of crowds. Not "divided" but one with all in God's Love. For one learns to be a Hearer who is No-Hearer, and one learns to forget all words and listen only to the One Word which seems to be No-Word. One opens the inner door of his heart to the infinite silences of the Spirit out of whose abysses love wells up without fail and gives itself to all. In His silence, the meaning of every sound is finally clear. Only in His silence can the truth of words be distinguished, not in their separateness, but in their pointing to the central unity of Love. All words then say one thing only: that *all is Love.*

Heidegger has said that our relation to what is closest to us is always confused and without vigor. What is closer to us than the solitude which is the ground of our being? It is always there. For that precise reason it is always ignored; for when we begin to think of it we are uncomfortable, we make an "object" of it, and our relation to it is falsified. And truly, we are so close to ourselves that there is really no "relation" to the ground of our own being. Can we not simply *be* ourselves without thinking about it? This is true solitude.

Is it true to say that one goes into solitude to "get at the root of existence"? It would be better simply to say that in solitude one is at the root. He who is alone and is conscious of what his solitude means, finds himself simply in the ground of life. He is "in Love." He is in love with all, with everyone, with everything. He is not surprised at this, and he is able to live with disconcerting and unexciting reality which has no explanation. He lives, then, as a seed planted in the ground. As Christ said, the seed in the ground must die. To be as a seed in the ground of one's life is to dissolve in that ground in order to become fruitful. One disappears into Love, in order to "be Love." But this fruitfulness is beyond any planning and any understanding of man. To be "fruitful" in this sense, one must forget every idea of fruitfulness or productivity and merely *be.* One's fruitfulness is at once an act of faith and an act of doubt: doubt of all that one has hitherto seen in oneself, and faith in what one cannot possibly imagine for oneself. The "doubt" dissolves our ego-identity. Faith gives us life in Christ, according to St. Paul's word: "I live, now not I, but Christ lives in me" (Galatians 2:20). To accept this is impossible unless one has profound hope in the incomprehensible fruitfulness that emerges from the dissolution of our ego in the ground of being and of Love. Such a hope is not the product of human reason, it is a secret gift of grace. It sustains us with divine and hidden aid. To accept our own dissolution would be inhuman if we did not at the same time accept the wholeness and completeness of everything in God's Love. We accept our emptying because we realize that our very emptiness is fulfillment and plentitude. In our emptiness the One Word is clearly spoken. It says, "I will never let go of you or desert you" (Hebrews 13:5) for I am your God, I am Love.

To leave this ground in order to plunge into the human and social process with multiple activities may well be only illusion, a purely imaginary fruitfuless.

Modern man believes he is fruitful and productive when his ego is aggresively affirmed, when he is visibly active, and when his action produces obvious results. But this activity is more and more filled with self-contradiction. The richest and most scientific culture in the world, potentially organized for unlimited production, is expending its huge power and wealth not on fruitfulness but on instruments of destruction. In such condition, even though men sincerely desire peace, their desire is only an illusion which cannot find fulfillment. Such men live in perpetual self-defeat.

To rebel against this self-defeat by a morbid self-imprisonment in the disillusioned ego would be a merely false solitude. Solitude is not withdrawal from ordinary life. It is not apart from, above, "better than" ordinary life; on the contrary, solitude is the very ground of ordinary life. It is the very ground of that simple, unpretentious, fully human activity by which we quietly earn our daily living and share our experiences with a few intimate friends. But we must learn to know and accept this ground of our being. To most people, though it is always there, it is unthinkable and unknown. Consequently their life has no center and no foundation. It is dispersed in a pretense of "togetherness" in which there is no real meaning. Only when our activity proceeds out of the ground in which we have consented to be dissolved does it have the divine fruitfulness of love and grace. Only then does it really reach others in true communion. Often our need for others is not love at all, but only the need to be sustained in our illusions, even as we sustain others in theirs. But when we have renounced these illusions, then we can certainly go out to others in true compassion. It is in solitude that illusions finally dissolve. But one must work hard to see that they do not reshape themselves in some worse form, peopling our solitude with devils disguised as angels of light. Love, simplicity and compassion protect us against this. He who is truly alone truly finds in himself the heart of compassion with which to love not only this man or that, but all men. He sees them all in the One who is the Word of God, the perfect manifestation of God's love, Jesus Christ.

XI

Preface to the

Vietnamese Edition

of

NO MAN

IS AN ISLAND

September 1966

THOMAS MERTON

KHÔNG AI
là một
HÒN ĐẢO

I

THANH-BẰNG dịch

Thomas Merton said in 1965 that his retirement to the hermitage presaged a withdrawal from contemporary events and issues. yet his compassion, his interest, his sense of justice prevented his ever truly withdrawing into an observant but mute solitude. One of the issues to which he turned his attention in the mid-60s was the Vietnamese War and his writings reflect his engrossment with this problem. "The agony of the Vietnamese conflict," as he and others described it, prompted him to express himself in print. The prolongation of the war heightened this feeling of agony and caused him increasingly to empathize and sympathize with the Vietnamese people. In addition to voicing his protest against what he came to feel was an unjust war, a war of "tragic stupidity," he felt it especially necessary to kindle in the American people a sense of kinship with those victimized by the war. He purposely called the paean he wrote after meeting the exiled Buddhist monk, Thich Nhat Hanh, in 1966, "Nhat Hanh is my Brother." This tribute, much reprinted and translated, was first published in August in Jubilee.

One month later Merton wrote a preface for a Vietnamese edition of a book from the 50s, No Man is an Island. *This book, similar to the earlier* Seeds of Contemplation, *originally called* Notes and Sentences *by Merton to describe it accurately as a series of rather short reflections, published in the United States in 1955, seemed appropriate as a follow-up to* Seeds *for publication in South Vietnam. Not one of Merton's favorites (he rated it "Good" but not "Better"), it had been modestly popular and, as Merton said in his preface, seemed suitable during a war which brought out "as clearly as anything else" that no man is an island. Written in a period of peace, it seemed viable in a time of war. In fact, Merton's prologue to the first edition had stated: "No matter how ruined man and his world may seem to be . . . his very humanity continues to tell him that life has a meaning." It was this thought, along with the idea that man cannot exist alone, that Merton forwarded in this preface, his only direct statement to the Vietnamese people.*

The edition, Không ai là Môt Hōn Dáo, *was published in Saigon by Phòng Trào Ván Hóa in 1967 with the preface printed in English. This version is taken from the last corrected draft found among Merton's papers, but he had revised it, had mimeographed it, and apparently had made some late changes in the text sent to Saigon for publication. These differences are indicated in footnotes. Merton did not rework the preface for publication in the United States, but it was included in the posthumous collection,* Thomas Merton on Peace, *introduced by Gordon Zahn and published in 1971. This version, the only one previously available in the United States, does not contain the changes made in the Vietnamese "English" version. The essay was omitted from the British abridgement published in 1976.*

The expression "No man is an island," which is now almost proverbial in the English language, comes from the meditation of a seventeenth century English Christian poet, John Donne. In the midst of the new optimistic individualism of the Renaissance he pointed out that it was an illusion for man to imagine himself perfectly and completely autonomous in himself, as if he were able to exist independently from his relation to other men and other living beings. This intuition was brought home to the poet by the fact of death. Hearing the bell toll for the funeral of a dead man, he reflected that there is one death for all and when the bell tolls "it tolls for thee."

Death is a silent yet eloquent teacher of truth. Death is a teacher that speaks openly and yet is [not] easily heard.[1] Death is very much present in our modern world: and yet it has become an enigma to that world. Instead of understanding death, it would seem that our world simply multiplies it. Death becomes a huge, inscrutable *quantity*.[2] The mystery of death, more terrible and sometimes more cruel than ever, remains incomprehensible to men who, though they know they must die, retain a grim and total attachment to individual life as if they could be physically inde-structible.

Perhaps it is this failure to understand and to face the fact of death that helps beget so many wars and so much violence. As if men, attached to individual bodily life, thought they could protect themselves against death by inflicting it on others.

Death cannot be understood without *compassion*. Compassion teaches me that when my brother dies, I too die. Compassion teaches me that my brother and I are one. That if I love my brother, then my love benefits my own life as well, and if I hate my brother and seek to destroy him, I destroy myself also. The desire to kill is like the desire to attack another with an ingot of red hot iron: I have to pick up the incandescent metal and burn my own hand while burning the other. Hate itself is the seed of death in my own heart, while it seeks the death of the other. Love is the seed of life in my own heart when it seeks the good of the other.

When this book was written, the author had in mind the per-sonal problems of men in a nation at peace. Now he is faced with the responsibility of introducing that same book to readers in a country that is burned, ravaged and torn to pieces by nearly twenty-five years of bitter war. What can be said in such a situation? It brings out as clearly as anything else the meaning of the title: "No man is an island." It is not difficult to sit in a quiet monastery and meditate on love, humility, mercy, inner silence, meditation and peace. But "No man is an island." A purely individualistic inner life, unconcerned for the suffering of others, is unreal. Therefore my meditation on love and peace must be realistically and intimately related to the fury of war, bloodshed, burning, destruction, killing that takes place on the other side of the earth.

This raises the great problem of responsibility in a world which has now become a vast unity, and in which everyone is involved in the lives and in the joys and sorrows of everyone else. There is war in Viet Nam. The power of my own country is engaged in the fight and in the destruction. Whatever may be the political issues, the rights and the wrongs, soldiers are fighting, men are killing each other, and their death tells me that "No man is an island." The war in Viet Nam is a bell tolling for the whole world, warning the whole world that war may spread everywhere, and violent death may sweep over the entire earth. And then perhaps men will ask: Why? Is there really a reason for this? Could these problems not be solved peacefully? Is there not some other answer than the shedding of so much blood? The burning and destruction of so many innocent people?

It is true, statesmen are concerned about this problem: they are sincerely asking these questions. But there never seems to be any answer other than to increase the killing, to multiply the dead. Can that be the answer of love, peace, mercy? If the answer is always brutal and destructive, then perhaps the question is being asked in the wrong terms. Or perhaps both the question and the answer are fundamentally dishonest. How can we know?

Without true compassion for others, without the sincere intention of seeing others as ourselves and treating others as we would want to be treated ourselves, we cannot ask and answer such questions in a really peaceful and honest manner. Violence rests on the assumption that the enemy and I are entirely different: the enemy is evil and I am good. The enemy must be destroyed and I must be saved. But love sees things differently. It sees that even the enemy suffers from the same sorrows and limitations that I do. That we both have the same hopes, the same needs, the same aspiration for a peaceful and harmless human life. And that death is the same for both of us. Then love may perhaps show me that my brother is not really my enemy and that war is both his enemy and mine. War is *our* enemy. Then peace becomes possible.

It is true, political problems are not solved by love and mercy. But the world of politics is not the only world, and unless political decisions rest on a foundation of something better and higher than politics, they can never do any real good for men. When a country has to be rebuilt after war, the passions and energies of war are no longer enough. There must be a new force, the power of love, the power of understanding and human compassion, the strength of selflessness and cooperation, and the creative dynamism of *the will to live and to build, and the will to forgive. The will for reconciliation.*

The principles given in this book are simple and more or less traditional. They are the principles derived from religious wisdom which, in the present case, is Christian.[3] But many of these principles run parallel to the ancient teachings of Buddhism. They are in fact in large part universal truths. They are truths with which, for centuries, man has slowly and with difficulty built a civilized world in the effort to make happiness possible, not merely by making life materially better, but by helping men *to understand and live their life more fruitfully.*

The key to this understanding is the truth that "No man is an island." A selfish life cannot be fruitful. It cannot be true. It contradicts the very nature of man. The dire effect of this contradiction cannot be avoided: where men live selfishly, in quest of brute power and lust and money, they destroy one another. The only way to change such a world is to change the thoughts and the desires of the men who live in it. The conditions of our world are simply an outward expression of our own thoughts and desires. The misfortune of Viet Nam today is that the war there expresses not merely the thoughts and desires of the people of Viet Nam but, unfortunately, the inner confusion of men in other nations in different parts of the earth. The sickness of the entire earth is now erupting in Viet Nam. But perhaps also the sickness of the entire earth may be cured there . . .

The pages of this book will not enable anyone to wage war and destroy other men. It was not written for that. But these pages may perhaps help some men to find peace even in the midst of war. Above all, they may help everyone who reads them to discover other ways of thinking, ways that will perhaps one day help them in building a world of peace. But for this to be possible, we must all believe in life and in peace. We must believe in the power of love. We must recognize that our being itself is grounded in love: that is to say that we come into being because we are loved and because we are meant to love others. The failure to believe this and to live accordingly creates instead a deep mistrust, a suspicion of others, a hatred of others, and a failure to love. When a man attempts to live by and for himself alone, he becomes a little "island" of hate, greed, suspicion, fear, desire. Then his whole outlook on life is falsified. All his judgments are affected by this untruth.[4] In order to recover the true perspective, which is that of love and compassion, he must once again learn, in simplicity, trust and peace, that "No man is an island."

XII

Preface to the Japanese Edition of

THE NEW MAN

October 1967

THE NEW MAN
by Thomas Merton

トマス・マートン

新しい人

木鎌安雄訳

Merton rated The New Man, *published in 1961, "Good," but by 1967 it had been translated only into Italian, Portuguese, and Spanish. Yet it was a work of spirituality, a work which Yasuwo Kikama who translated it into Japanese felt would have "a good effect on Japanese spiritualism." Merton replied that he was glad Kikama felt it would have meaning in Japan and responded immediately to his request for a third special preface for a Japanese edition. He wrote to Kikama in October after completing the preface: "As always, I feel very close to the Japanese people and am very grateful for your services in enabling me to communicate with them." This preface, this communication to the Japanese people, was the last special preface Merton wrote for a foreign edition.*

This version is taken from Merton's revised and corrected draft, the one which he sent to Kikama and the one which appeared in translation in the Japanese edition. Following his usual practice of adapting for publication in the United States, he began extensive rewriting in the spring of 1968. In April he had finished his revision, retitled the essay "Rebirth and the New Man in Christianity," and had copies mimeographed for distribution. There is no doubt that he meant to publish the essay, but his trips to Alaska, California, and then to Asia intervened and, at the time of his death in Bangkok in December 1968, he had yet to submit it for publication. The reworked and augmented version was finally published in Cistercian Studies *in 1978 and was included in the collection* Love and Living, *edited by Brother Patrick Hart and published in 1979. The version here is the one sent to Japan before Merton rewrote it for publication in the United States.*

"You must be born again!"

These mysterious and challenging words of Jesus Christ reveal the inner meaning of Christianity as life and dynamism. More than that, spiritual rebirth is the key to the aspirations of all the higher religions. By "higher religions" I mean those which, like Buddhism, Hinduism, Judaism, Islam and Christianity, are not content with the ritual tribal cults rooted in the cycle of the seasons and harvests. These "higher religions" answer a deeper need in man: a need that cannot be satisfied merely by the ritual celebration of man's oneness with nature—his joy in the return of spring! Man seeks to be liberated from mere natural necessity, from servitude to fertility and seasons, from the round of birth, growth and death. Man is not content with slavery to need: making his living, raising his family, and leaving a good name to his posterity. There is in the depths of man's heart a voice which says: "You must be born again."

What does this voice mean? It is hard to say. Sometimes it is merely an expression of weariness, a sense of failure, an awareness of wrong, a half-hopeless wish that one might get another chance, be born over again. One desires to begin a new life because the burden of the old has now become an unbearable accumulation of fatigue, mistakes, betrayals, disappointments. One longs for a new life because the old life is stale, unworthy, uninteresting, hopeless. One looks for a new way because all the familiar ways are a dead end.

Unfortunately, this weariness with the old, this longing for the new, is often just another trap of nature, another variation in the imprisonment we would like to escape. It may inspire us with bright hopes, and it may induce us to believe we have found a new answer: but then after a while, the same despair regains possession of our heart. Or else we simply fall back into the same old routine.

For modern man, the "old" is often paradoxically that which claims to be "new." Man in modern, technological society has begun to be callous and disillusioned. He has learned to suspect what claims to be new, to doubt all the "latest" in everything. He is drawn instinctively to the new, and yet he sees in it nothing but the same old sham. The specious glitter of newness, the pretended creativity of a society in which youthfulness is commercialized and the young are old before they are twenty, fills some hearts with utter despair. There seems to be no way to find any real change. "The more things change," says a French proverb, "the more they are the same."

Yet in the deepest ground of our being we still hear the insistent voice which tells us: "You must be born again."

There is in us an instinct for newness, for renewal, for a liberation of creative power. We seek to awaken in ourselves a force which really changes our lives from within. And yet the same instinct tells us that this change is a recovery of that which is deepest, most original, most personal in ourselves. To be born again is not to become somebody else, *but to become ourselves.*

The deepest spiritual instinct in man is this urge of inner truth which demands that he be faithful to himself: to his deepest and most original potentialities. yet at the same time, in order to become oneself, one must die. That is to say, in order to become one's true self, the false self must die. In order for the inner self to appear the outer self must disappear: or at least become secondary, unimportant.

How does one do this? In modern secular life, men resort to many expedients. If you have a great deal of money and can afford a long analysis—and can find an especially good psychoanalyst—it is possible that you may arrive at a psychological breakthrough and liberation, a recovery of authenticity and independence. But in reality, psychoanalysis and psychiatry tend more to workable compromises which enable us to function without having to undergo an impossible transformation. We are not born again, we simply learn to put up with ourselves. Well, that is already something!

More usually the desperation of modern man drives him to seek a kind of new life and rebirth in mass movements, sometimes of an extremist character, sometimes messianic and political quasi-religions. In these he tries to forget himself, in dedication to a more or less idealistic cause. But he is not born again, because true rebirth is a spiritual and religious transformation, far beyond the level of an ideology or a political "cause."

111

In the Gospel of St. John, we read the conversation in which Jesus speaks of man's new birth. It is a conversation with one of the leading scholars of the Jews who came by night to speak with Jesus in secret. Nicodemus, the scholar, begins by saying that he recognizes Jesus as a true master sent by God. Jesus dismisses this statement as of no importance. He does not seek the veneration of disciples. He says there is something of much more crucial importance than being the disciple of a spiritual master, however great. A man must be born again, or in a better translation, "born from above." (John 3:3)

Nicodemus, the scholar, asks in bewilderment: "How can a grown man be born? Can he go back into his mother's womb and be born again?" This is a natural question of a man who knows life in the world and is suspicious of spiritual and "mystical" delusions. We cannot reverse our course. We cannot really change (he thinks): all we can do is find some better ideal, some discipline, some new practices or ideas which will enable us to live the same life with less trouble and fewer mistakes.

But Jesus contradicts this in very forceful language.

Unless a man is born through water and the Spirit
He cannot enter the Kingdom of God.
What is born of flesh is flesh;
What is born of Spirit is Spirit.
Do not be surprised when I say
You must be born from above.
The wind blows where ever it pleases;
You hear its sound
But you cannot tell where it comes from or where it is going.
That is how it is with all who are born of the Spirit.

(John 3:5-8)

In other words, what Jesus speaks of is an entirely new kind of birth. It is a birth which gives definitive meaning to life. The first birth, of the body, is a preparation for the second birth, the spiritual awakening of mind and heart. This is not to be confused with the awakening of rational consciousness which makes a human being responsible for his actions as an individual. It is a deep spiritual consciousness which takes man beyond the level of his individual ego. This deep consciousness, to which we are initiated by spiritual rebirth, is an awareness that we are not merely our everyday selves but we are also one with One who is beyond all human and individual self-limitation.

To be born again is to be born beyond egoism, beyond selfishness, beyond individuality, in Christ. To be born of flesh is to be born into the human race with its fighting, its hatreds, its loves, its passions, its struggles, its appetites. To be born of spirit is to be born into God (or the Kingdom of God) beyond hatred, beyond struggle, in peace, love, joy, self-effacement, service, gentleness, humility, strength.

How does this birth take place? By the water of baptism (which may well be a baptism solely of "desire," that is to say a spiritual awakening in which the spirit is "washed" and renewed in God) and by the coming of the Spirit which is in Jesus' words, as unpredictable and as unexpected as the wind. The Spirit moves constantly over the face of the whole earth, and though He makes use of human messengers, He is not bound to them or limited to them. He can act without them.

At this point we must observe that the rebirth of which Christ speaks is not a single event but a continuous dynamic of inner renewal. Certainly, sacramental baptism, the "birth by water" can be given only once. But birth in the Spirit happens many times in a man's life, as he passes through successive stages of spiritual development. A false and superficial view of Christianity assumes that it is enough to be baptized with water and to observe certain ethical and ritual prescriptions in order to guarantee for oneself a happy life in the other world. But this is only a naïve view of Christianity. True Christianity is growth in the life of the Spirit, a deepening of the new life, a continuous rebirth, in which the exterior and superficial life of the ego-self is discarded like an old snake skin and the mysterious, invisible self of the Spirit becomes more present and more active. The true Christian rebirth is a renewed transformation, a "passover" in which man is progressively liberated from selfishness and not only grows in love but in some sense "becomes love." The perfection of the new birth is reached where there is no more selfishness, there is only love. In the language of the mystics, there is no more ego-self, there is only Christ; self no longer acts, only the Spirit acts in pure love. The perfect illumination is then the illumination of Love shining by itself. To become completely transparent and allow Love to shine by itself, is the maturity of the "New Man."

Nicodemus, the scholar, could not understand. He had an active ego-centered view of perfection. His life was based on the observance of strict religious law, and the understanding of this law depended on correct interpretation. Thus there was need for many experts and trained legal minds to help everyone keep the law in its every detail. Jesus was speaking of something quite different: of a Spirit who came like the wind, invisible, unpredictable, and transformed one's whole life.

"You must be born of the Spirit."

It is not enough to remain the same "self," the same individual ego, with a new set of activities and new lot of religious practices. One must be born of the Spirit who is free, and who teaches the inmost depths of the heart by taking that heart to Himself, by making Himself one with our heart, by creating for us, invisibly, a new identity: by being Himself that identity. (I Corinthians 2:6-16, II Corinthians 3:12-18, Romans 8:14-17, etc.)

Nicodemus thought this was impossible. Jesus then rebuked him, because he claimed to be a scholar and an expert in those truths which explain the meaning of man's existence: and yet he did not know this elementary truth of religious existence. The life of man has no meaning if he is simply born in the flesh, born into the human race, without being born of the Spirit, or born into God.

The famous Japanese Zen scholar, Daisetz Suzuki, had a deep appreciation for this Christian idea of the "birth of God" in man, as expressed by the Rhenish mystics. In this Dr. Suzuki was much less like Nicodemus than many Christian scholars: he penetrated one essential aspect of Christianity and saw its true meaning. His Zen doubtless gave him this understanding. This is perhaps also true of Kitaro Nishida, one of the great philosophers of our century, who likewise saw the deeper dimensions of Christianity.

But the argument between Christ and Nicodemus is renewed in every century. Each age has the answer of Nicodemus: "How can a man be born again? How can he enter again into his mother's womb?" In other words, every age has official ideological answers that seek to evade the necessity of the divine birth. The human birth is enough: then one need only to seek a political, or ethical, or doctrinal, or philosophical answer. Or one needs only to seek a new drug, a new pleasure, a new love affair, a new experience. Even the Christians themselves have at times followed Nicodemus rather than Christ, when they have identified Christianity with a given social or political or economic structure, or with a mere ideological system. But whenever a certain group of Christians has done this, then other men, strangers and new converts, have come in answer to the call of the Spirit. These others have been more attentive to the quiet secret voice speaking softly as the wind. They have been willing to risk everything in order to be born again, not in the flesh but in God.

I as a western man send you this book and this message, to you my brothers and sisters in a distant country. We of the west have not always been worthy of the gift of faith that was given us. We have perhaps misrepresented Christ, and given a strange, distorted idea of Him to the other peoples of the earth. Do not judge by us, but judge by His word and His Spirit. Do not let anything about us deter you from looking deeper into this mysterious problem and this invitation, to become new men and new women.

The message of Christ, the message of the new life, came to the Far East together with a new civilization. But the two are not the same. To become a new man does not mean to become a western man, a europeanized or americanized man. What is new about this? It is little more than putting on new clothes and learning to struggle with a different set of problems. It means learning a new kind of confusion and unhappiness. That is not the message of Christ!

This book was first written for western readers who are presumed to know about Christianity. Hence it does not attempt to explain the rudiments of Christian belief.

However it does insist on an elementary aspect of Christianity which is often neglected by the activism of the west. The west has lived for thousands of years under the sign of the aggressive Titan, Prometheus, the fire-stealer, the man of power who defies heaven in order to get what he himself desires. The west has lived under this sign of will, the love of power, action and domination. Hence western Christianity has often been associated with a spiritual will-to-power and an instinct for organization and authority. This has taken good forms, in devotion to works of education, healing the sick, building schools, order and organization in religion itself. But even this good side of activism has tended toward an overemphasis on will, on action, on conquest, on "getting things done" and this in turn has resulted in a sort of religious restlessness, pragmatism, and the worship of visible results.

There is another essential aspect of Christianity: the interior, the silent, the contemplative, in which hidden wisdom is more important than practical organizational science, and in which love replaces the will to get visible results, The New Man must not be a one sided and aggressive activist: he must also have depth, he must be able to be silent, to listen to the secret voice of the Spirit. He must renounce his own will to dominate, and let the Spirit act secretly in and through him. This aspect of Christianity will perhaps be intelligible to those in an Asian culture who are familiar with the deeper aspects of their own religious tradition. For the religions of Asia also have long sought to liberate man from imprisonment in a half real external existence, in order to initiate him into the full and complete reality of an inner peace which is secret and beyond explanation.

We are all called to become fully real, not by intensifying our passions, conquests and experiences "in the flesh" but by attaining to a reality beyond the limitations of selfishness, in the Spirit.

We must be born again.

That is the subject which is discussed in this meditation on the Christian theme of the New Man.

Appendix 1

Original Draft
for the
Preface
to the
Japanese Edition
of
THOUGHTS IN
SOLITUDE

This book says nothing that has not already been said better by the wind in the pine trees. Its pages seek nothing more than to echo the silence and the peace that is "heard" when the rain wanders freely among the hills and forests. But what can the wind say where there is no hearer? There is then a deeper silence: the silence in which the Hearer is No-Hearer. That deeper silence, too, is part of this book.

These pages do not attempt to convey any special information, or to answer deep philosophical questions about life. True, they do concern themselves with questions about life. But can a book really answer such questions? I think not. So these pages do not pretend to do the reader's thinking for him. On the contrary, they invite him to listen for himself. They do not merely speak to him, they remind him that he is a Hearer.

But who is the Hearer?

Beyond the Hearer, is there perhaps No-Hearer?

Who is this No-Hearer?

For such questions there are no intelligble answers. The only answer is the Hearing itself. The proper climate for such Hearing is solitude.

The world is shrinking. There is less and less space in which men can be alone. It is said that if we go on increasing at our present rate, then in six hundred and fifty years there will only be one square foot left for every person. Even then, there will be one square foot of solitude. Or is that right? Is each person a separate solitude of his own? Or is there One Solitude in which all persons are at once together and alone? Again, how shall such a question be answered? The answer is not found in words, but by living on a certain level of consciousness. This book is, then, concerned with a spiritual climate, an atmosphere, a landscape of the mind, a level of consciousness: the peace, the silence of aloneness in which the Hearer listens, and the Hearing is No-Hearing.

Christianity is a religion of the Word. But we sometimes forget that the Word emerges first of all from silence. Where there is no silence, then the One Word which God speaks is not truly heard. Then only "words" are heard. Where there are many words, we lose consciousness of the fact that there is really only One Word.

The One Word which God speaks is Himself. His speaking and His hearing are One. So silent is His speech that, to our way of thinking, His speech is no speech, His hearing is No-Hearing. In His silence all words are spoken and all words are heard. Only in this silence do they have coherence and meaning. Yet we draw them out of silence in order to separate them from one another, to make them distinct, to give them a unique sound by which we can discern them. This is necessary. Yet in all these sounds there remains the hidden, secret power of silence which is the power of God. "When all things were enveloped in quiet silence," says the Book of Wisdom (18:14), "and when the night had reached the mid-point in its course, from the height of the heavens Thy all powerful Word leaped down from the royal throne." By the action that takes place in life and history the secret non-action of Word and power manifest their reality.

Even though one may be a learned man and may have profound knowledge of many subjects, and many "words", this is of no value, it has no central meaning, if the One Word has not been shared. That One Word is heard only in the silence and solitude of the empty heart, the heart that is at peace, detached, free, without care. In the language of Christianity, this freedom is the realm of faith.

When the Christian faith is made to appear very complicated, it seems to consist of numerous strange doctrines, all of which impart information and seem to answer all possible questions about the after life, and about the means to attain to happiness in heaven. While these doctrines may be very true, they cannot be understood if we think that the only object of faith is information communicated in many complex doctrines. In fact, the object of faith is God. And though the revealed doctrines about Him are true, yet what they tell us of Him is not fully adequate. They must converge upon Him as the spokes of a wheel converge upon a central hub. They are window frames through which the One light enters our houses. The window frame is precise and distinct: yet what we really see is the light itself, which is diffuse and all-pervading, so that it is everywhere and nowhere. No mind can comprehend God's reality, as it is in itself, and if we approach

Him we must advance not only by knowing but by not-knowing. We must seek to communicate with Him not only by words, but above all by silence, in which there is only the One Word, and the One Word is endless silence.

Where is silence? Where is solitude?

Ultimately, these cannot be found anywhere except in the ground of our own being. Where, in the silent depths, there is no more distinction between the I and the Not-I. There is perfect peace. There we encounter God, when no eye can see, and in whom, as St. Paul says, "we live and move and have our being" (Acts 17:28). In Him, too, we find solitude, as St. John of the Cross said, we find that the All and the Nothing encounter one another and are the Same.

If there is no silence beyond and within the words of doctrine, there is no religion, only a religious ideology. For religion goes beyond words and actions, and attains to the ultimate truth only in silence. Where this silence is lacking, where there are only the "many words" and not the One Word, then there is much bustle and activity, but no peace, no deep thought, no understanding, no inner quiet. Where there is no peace, there is no light. The mind that is hyper-active seems to itself to be awake and productive, but it is dreaming. Only in silence and solitude, in the quiet of worship, the reverent peace of prayer, the adoration in which the entire ego-self silences and abases itself in the presence of the Invisible God, only in these "activities" which are "non-actions" does the spirit truly wake from the dream of a multifarious and confused existence.

Precisely because of this, modern western man is afraid of solitude. He is unable to be alone, to be silent. And he is communicating his spiritual and mental sickness to men of the East. Asia is tempted by the violence and activism of the West, and is gradually losing hold of its traditional respect for silent wisdom. Therefore, it is all the more necessary, at this time to rediscover the climate of solitude and silence: not that everyone can go apart and live alone. But in moments of silence, of meditation, of enlightenment and peace, one learns to be silent and alone everywhere. One learns to live in the atmosphere of solitude even in the midst of crowds. For one learns to be a Hearer who is No-Hearer, and one learns to forget all words and listen only to the One Word which seems to be No-Word. In His silence, the meaning of every sound is finally clear. Only in His silence can the truth of words be distinguished.

True, there are a few men whose mission is to live alone, to be Hearers rather than Speakers. The author of this book is one of them. The book itself is simply a fragment of on-going solitude. It was written mostly in a small wooden hut in the woods, near a monastery. That was more than ten years ago. But the solitary life continues much the same, except that while the book was written in a wooden hut in the valley, the preface is written in a concrete hut on a hill. The hills are the same, the woods are the same, the trees are the same. The silence is the same, and the only difference is that the monastery bells come from a different direction, and the author is older.

Certainly the author does not spend all his time alone. There is work to be done, and books are written. Conferences are given, people ask advice. A solitary is not absent from the rest of men, and a solitude that merely excluded other men would be pure illusion. Yet a solitary prefers the silence and solitude of the woods, and he is most awake, most true to his calling. When he is with no one. Nevertheless he can share with others what he considers most precious: the climate of emptiness in which he lives. That is all this book claims to do.

Heidegger has said that our relation to what is closest to us is always confused and without vigor. What is closer to us than the solitude which is the ground of our being? It is always there. For that precise reason it is always ignored, for when we begin to think of it we are uncomfortable, we make an "object" of it, and our relation to it is wrong. And truly, we are so close to ourselves that there is really no "relation" to the ground of ourselves. Can we not simply *be* ourselves without thinking about it? This is true solitude.

As I said, the book is nothing but a fragment. Other things have been seen and said, sometimes noted down, in the silences since this was written. Perhaps a few lines from a more recent notebook might throw light on the meaning of solitude. These words were jotted down a few days ago, but they could have formed part of this book. They are not out of place here:

"Is it true to say that one goes into solitude to get at the root of existence?" It would be better simply to say that in solitude one *is* at the root. He who is alone, and is conscious of what his solitude means, finds himself simply in the ground of life. He is not surprised at it, and he is able to live with this disconcerting and unexciting reality, which has no explanation. He lives, then, as a seed planted in the ground. As Christ said, the seed in the ground must die. To be as a seed in the ground of one's very life is to dissolve in that ground in order to become fruitful. But this fruitfulness is beyond any planning and any understanding of man. To be "fruitful" in this sense, one must not forget every idea of fruitfulness or productivity, and merely *be*. One's fruitfulness is at once an act of faith and an act of doubt: doubt of all that one has hitherto seen in oneself, and faith in what one cannot possibly imagine for oneself. The "doubt" dissolves our ego-identity. Faith gives us life in Christ, according to St. Paul's word: "I live, now not I, but Christ lives in me." (Galatians 2:20). To accept this is impossible unless one has profound hope in the incomprehensible fruitfulness that emerges from this dissolution of our age in the ground of our being. Such a hope is not the product of human reason, it is a secret gift of grace. It sustains us with divine and hidden aid. To accept our own dissolution would be inhuman if we did not at the same time accept the wholeness and completeness of everything in God. We accept our emptying because we realize that our very emptiness is fulfillment and plenitude. In our emptiness the One word is clearly spoken.

To leave this ground in order to plunge into the human and social process with multiple activities, may well be only an illusion, a purely imaginary fruitfulness.

Modern man believes he is fruitful and productive when his ego is aggressively affirmed, when he is visibly active, and when his action produces obvious results. But this activity is more and more fulfilled with self-contradiction. The richest and most scientific culture in the world, potentially organized for unlimited production, is expending its huge force and wealth not on fruitfulness but on instruments of destruction. In such conditions, even though men sincerely desire peace, their desire is only an illusion which cannot find fulfillment. Such men live in perpetual self-defeat.

To rebel against this self-defeat by a morbid self-imprisonment in the disillusioned ego, would be a merely false solitude. Solitude is not withdrawal from ordinary life. It is not apart from, above "better than" ordinary life, on the contrary, solitude is the very ground of ordinary life. It is the very ground of that simple, unpretentious, fully human activity by which we quietly earn our daily living and share our experience with a few intimate friends. But we must learn to know and accept this ground of our being. To most people, though it is always there, it is unthinkable and unknown. Consequently their life has no center and no foundation. It is dispersed in a pretense of "togetherness" in which there is no real meaning. Only when our activity proceeds out of the ground in which we have consented to be dissolved, does it have the divine fruitfulness of love and grace. Only then does it really reach others in true communion. Often our need for others is not love at all, but only the need to be sustained in our illusions, even as we sustain others in theirs. But when we have renounced these illusions, then we can certainly go out to others in true compassion. It is in solitude that illusions finally dissolve. But one must work hard to see that they do not re-shape themselves in some worse form peopling our solitude with devils disguised as angels of light. Love, simplicity and compassion protect us against this. He who is truly alone truly finds in himself the heart of compassion with which to love not only this man or that, but all men. He sees them all in the One who is the Word, of God, Jesus Christ.

Appendix 2

Thomas Merton's

GRAPH

Evaluating

His Own Books

1967

Best

Better

Good

Less Good

Poor.

Very Poor

Awful.

Thirty Poems
Mass in Divided Key

Figures for Apocalypse.
Exile Ends in Glory
Seven Storey Mtn

Seeds of Contemplation
Waters of Silve

Tears of Blind Lions
What are these Wounds
Ascent to Truth
Sign of Jonas

Graph of my work. Feb 6. 1967

← New Fran Fox

← Emblems (Ox?)

Bread in Wilderness
Cost of the Follies
No Room in the Blood
Living Bread
Stormy Islands
School hill
Thoughts in latitude
Spiritual Freedom & Meditation
Wisdom of Desert
Disputed Questions
New Seeds.
Life + Monism.
Seeds of Destruction
Chuang Tzu
Seasons of Celebration
Kauai
Conjectures

Appendix 3

CHECKLIST

BIBLIOGRAPHY

OF

THOMAS MERTON'S

MAJOR WRITINGS

Arranged chronologically by original publication date
Including books, pamphlets, translations, and limited editions

B	= British Edition	H	= Hungarian	RUM	= Rumanian
CAT	= Catalan	IND	= Indonesian	R	= Russian
CH	= Chinese (Mandarin)	I	= Italian	SC	= Serbo-Croatian
CZ	= Czech	J	= Japanese	SINH	= Sinhalese
D	= Danish	K	= Korean	SLOV	= Slovene
F	= French	N	= Netherlandic	S	= Spanish
G	= German	PL	= Polish	SW	= Swedish
GK	= Greek	P	= Portuguese	TAMIL	= Tamil
				V	= Vietnamese

Note: Dutch and *Flemish* editions are listed under *Netherlandic.*

TITLE	TYPE	PUBLISHER	YEAR
Thirty poems I	Book/poems	New Directions *Collected Poems*	1944 1977
A man in the divided sea B, I	Book/poems	New Directions *Collected poems*	1946 1977
The soul of the apostolate, by J.-B. Chautard	Translation	Gethsemani Image pb	1946 1961
Guide to Cistercian life	Pamphlet	Gethsemani	1948
Cistercian contemplatives	Pamphlet	Gethsemani	1948
Figures for an apocalypse B, G, I, PL, P, S	Book/poems	New Directions *Collected poems*	1948 1977

The spirit of simplicity	Book/translation	Gethsemani	1948
		TM on St. Bernard	1980
Exile ends in glory B, F, G, I, N, S	Book/biography	Bruce	1948
The seven storey mountain B, B2, B3, CAT, CZ, D, F, G, I, J, K, N, PL, P, S, SW	Book/autobiography	Harcourt, Brace Garden City reprint Signet pb Signet pb Image pb Harvest pb Octagon (library ed.)	1948 1951 1952 1955 1970 1978 1979
What is contemplation? B, B2, G, I, P, S	Pamphlet	Notre Dame Templegate Templegate	1948 1960 1970
Seeds of contemplation B, B2, CH, D, F, G, I, J, J2, K, N, PL, P, S, SW, SW2, V	Book	New Directions Dell pb Greenwood reprint	1949 1953 1979
Gethsemani magnificat	Pamphlet	Gethsemani	1949
The tears of the blind lions B, I	Book/poems	New Directions *Collected poems*	1949 1977
The waters of Siloe B, B2, F, I, N, P, S	Book	Harcourt, Brace Garden City reprint Image pb Harvest pb	1949 1951 1962 1979
Selected poems *(British edition)*	Book/poems	Hollis & Carter	1950
What are these wounds? B, F, G, I, N, P, S	Book/biography	Bruce	1950
A balanced life of prayer I, S	Pamphlet	Gethsemani	1951

The ascent to truth B, B2, F, G, I, N, P, S	Book	Harcourt, Brace Compass pb	1951 1959
Devotions to *St. John of the Cross*	Pamphlet	Gethsemani	1953
The sign of Jonas B, B2, D, F, G, I, PL, P, S	Book/journal	Harcourt, Brace Image pb Harvest pb	1953 1956 1979
Bread in the wilderness B, B2, F, G, I, N, P, S, SW	Book	New Directions ND trade & pb Liturgical Press pb	1953 1960 1971
The last of the fathers B, F, P, S	Book/biography	Harcourt, Brace Greenwood reprint	1954 1970
No man is an island B, B2, CAT, F, G, G2,I, N, PL, P, SC, S, V	Book	Harcourt, Brace Dell pb Image pb Harvest pb	1955 1957 1967 1978
The living bread B, B2, F, G, I, N, PL, P, S	Book	Farrar, Straus Dell Pb Farrar, Straus	1956 1959 1980
Praying the Psalms B, B2, F, IND, I, PL, SINH, TAMIL	Pamphlet	Liturgical Press	1956
Silence in heaven B, F, G, SW	Book	Crowell	1956
Marthe, Marie et Lazare (French edition) P Included in *Thomas Merton on* *St. Bernard*	Book	Desclée de Brouwer Cistercian Pubs.	1956 1980

Basic principles of monastic spirituality B, G, J, P	Pamphlet	Gethsemani *Monastic journey*	1957 1977
The silent life B, B2, F, G, I, N, P, S	Book	Farrar, Straus Dell pb Noonday pb	1957 1959 1975
The strange islands B	Book/poems	New Directions *Collected poems*	1957 1977
The tower of Babel S	Limited edition	New Directions *Strange islands* *Collected poems*	1957 1957 1977
Monastic peace F, P, S	Pamphlet	Gethsemani *Monastic journey*	1958 1977
Thoughts in solitude B, B2, CH, G, I, J, PL, P, S	Book	Farrar, Straus Dell pb Image pb Noonday pb	1958 1961 1968 1976
Prometheus/a meditation F, S	Limited edition	U.K.-King Library *Behavior of Titans* *Merton reader* *Raids/unspeakable*	1958 1961 1962 1966
Nativity kerygma	Limited edition	Gethsemani *Merton reader*	1958 1962
The Christmas sermons of B1. *Guerric of Igny* G	Limited edition	Gethsemani	1959
What Ought I to do? P1	Limited edition	Stamperia del Santuccio	 1959
The secular journal *of Thomas Merton* B, B2, F, G, I, P	Book/journal	Farrar, Straus Dell pb Image pb Noonday pb	1959 1960 1969 1977

Selected poems *of Thomas Merton* G, I, P, S	Book/poems	New Directions ND Enlarged edition *Collected poems*	1959 1967 1977
The solitary life	Limited edition	Stamperia del Santuccio	 1960
The Ox-mountain *parable of Meng Tzu*	Limited edition	Stamperia del Santuccio	 1960
Spiritual direction *and meditation* B, B2, F, G, H, I, P	Book	Liturgical Press	1960
God is my life	Book	Reynal	1960
Disputed questions B, B2, F, I, P, S	Book	Farrar, Straus Mentor pb Noonday pb	1960 1965 1976
The wisdom of the desert B, B2, F, N	Book/editor	New Directions ND pb	1960 1970
The behavior of Titans F	Book	New Directions	1961
The new man B, B2, F, GK, I, J, P, S	Book	Farrar, Straus Mentor pb Noonday pb	1961 1963 1978
New Seeds *of contemplation* B, B2, F, G, I, P, SC, S	Book	New Directions New Directions pb	1961 1972
Original child bomb S	Limited edition	New Directions *Collected poems*	1962 1977
Hagia Sophia	Limited edition	Stamperia del Santuccio *Emblems/fury* *Collected poems* Stamperia del Santuccio	 1962 1963 1977 1978

Clement of Alexandria	Pamphlet/	New Directions translation	1962
Loretto and Gethsemani	Pamphlet	Gethsemani	(1962)
A Thomas Merton reader	Book/ anthology	Harcourt, Brace Image pb	1962 1974
Life and holiness B, CAT, F, G, H, I, J, K, N, P, RUM, SLOV, S	Book	Herder & Herder Image pb	1963 1964
Breakthrough to peace P	Book/editor	New Directions	1963
Emblems of a season of fury G, I	Book/poems	New Directions *Collected poems*	1963 1977
The solitary life: Guigo the Carthusian B2	Pamphlet Limited edition	Stanbrook Abbey Banyan press	1963 1977
Seeds of destruction F, I, P, S	Book	Farrar, Straus Macmillan pb Noonday pb	1964 1967 1980
Redeeming the time (Abridged British edition with added material) P		Burns & Oates	1966
The black revolution (excerpt from Seeds of destruction) Paperbacks CAT, F, G, I, S			
Come to the mountain	Pamphlet	St. Benedict's	1964
Reprinted under title *Cistercian life* CH, F, IND, S	Pamphlet	Cistercian Pubs.	1974
Gandhi on non-violence P	Book/editor	New Directions	1965

The way of Chuang Tzu B, F, G, N, P, S	Book/ translation	New Directions New Directions pb	1965 1969
Seasons of celebration B, F, I, I2, P, S	Book	Farrar, Straus Noonday pb	1965 1977
Raids on the unspeakable B, F, S, S2	Book	New Directions	1966
Monastic life at Gethsemani	Pamphlet	Gethsemani	1966
Gethsemani/ a life of praise	Book/photographs	Gethsemani	1966
Conjectures of a guilty bystander B, B2, F, I, N, POL, P, S	Book/journal Image pb	Doubleday 1968	1966
A prayer of Cassiodorus	Limited edition/ translation	Stanbrook Abbey	1967
Mystics and Zen masters B, F, G, I, J, K, P	Book	Farrar, Straus Delta pb	1967 1969
Monks pond (4 issues)	Periodical/editor	Gethsemani	1968
Cables to the ace I	Book/poems	New Directions New Directions pb *Collected poems*	1968 1968 1977
Faith and violence F, I, I2	Book	Notre Dame	1968
Zen and the birds of appetite B, F, G, I, J, N, P, S	Book	New Directions New Directions pb	1968 1968
The true solitude	Gift book	Hallmark	1969
My argument with the Gestapo I	Book/novel	Doubleday New Directions pb	1969 1975

The climate of monastic prayer B, F, I, J, P, S	Book	Cistercian Pubs. Cistercian Pubs.	1969 1973

Also printed under title:

Contemplative prayer B, G, K, N	Book	Herder & Herder Image pb	1969 1971
The geography of Lograire I	Book/poems	New Directions New Directions pb *Collected poems*	1969 1969 1977
Early poems/1940-1942	Limited edition	Anvil Press *Collected poems*	1971 1977
Opening the Bible B, K, P, S	Book	Liturgical Press	1971
Contemplation in a world of action	Book	Doubleday Image pb	1971 1973
Thomas Merton on peace B	Book	McCall	1971

Revised as

The nonviolent alternative		Farrar, Straus	1980
Pasternak/Merton: six letters R	Limited edition	U.K.-King Library	1973
The Asian journal of Thomas Merton B, B2, G, I, P	Book/journal	New Directions New Directions pb	1973 1975
The jaguar and the moon, by Pablo Antonio Cuadra	Translation/poems	Unicorn Press	1974
He is risen	Book	Argus	1975
Ishi means man S	Book	Unicorn Press Unicorn Press pb 1976	1976

On the solitary life, by Guigo	Limited edition/ translation	Banyan Press	1977
The monastic journey B	Book	Sheed, Andrews Image pb	1977 1978
The collected poems of Thomas Merton B	Book/poems	New Directions *New Directions pb*	1977 *1980*
The Thomas Merton 1979 Appointment Calendar	Calendar/ drawings	Sheed, Andrews	1978
A catch of anti-letters, by Thomas Merton and Robert Lax	Book/letters	Sheed, Andrews	1978
The Thomas Merton 1980 Appointment Calendar	Calendar/ drawings	Andrews & McMeel	1979
Love and living B	Book	Farrar, Straus	1979
The nonviolent alternative	Book	Farrar, Straus	1980

Revised edition of *Thomas Merton on peace*

The Thomas Merton 1981 Appointment Calendar	Calendar/ photographs	Andrews & McMeel	1980
Geography of holiness	Book/photographs	Pilgrim Press	1980
Thomas Merton on St. Bernard	Book	Cistercian Pubs.	1980

F, P

Published in translation in 1956 in part as *Marthe, Marie et Lazare*

NOTES

Chapter 4.   Preface to the Argentine Edition of
            THE COMPLETE WORKS OF THOMAS MERTON.

1. *La Virgen Morena*, the dark-skinned Virgin, is a term in general use in Latin America and may refer specifically to representations of the Virgin veneratd by the inhabitants in various areas. Merton obviously found these vital and earthy representations more valid images than those of the North which he considered pale, languid, and insipid.

2. This passage, marked and underscored by Merton in his *New Testament*, has the marginal notation "Vocations = building" in Merton's handwriting. See *The New Testament;* a Revision of the Challoner-Reims version, edited by Catholic scholars under the patronage of the Episcopal Committee of the Confraternity of Christian Doctrine (New York, Catholic Book Publishing Company, 1950), pp. 252-253. The volume is housed in the "Marginialia Section" of the Thomas Merton Studies Center, Bellarmine College.

Chapter 5.   Preface to the Japanese Edition of
            THE SEVEN STOREY MOUNTAIN.

1. The word "source" was changed to "heart" in the published Japanese edition.

2. "Fury" was changed to "insensitivity" in the Japanese edition.

3. This paragraph was divided into two paragraphs after this sentence in the Japanese edition.

4. "Life" was changed to "existence" in the Japanese edition.

5. The word "Christendom" was changed to "Christianity" in the Japanese edition, a change which seems to make the sentence and Merton's meaning somewhat clearer.

6. Merton, whose spelling always retained some British vestiges, wrote the word "judgment" as "judgement" in both his original typescript version and in the mimeograph version. The spelling "judgement" was used in the Japanese edition, but changed to "judgment" in the *Queen's Work* version published in the United States.

7. The article "a" was deleted in the Japanese edition.

8. The last line of the Japanese edition reads "to One who lives and speaks in us both!"

Chapter 11.   Preface to the Vietnamese Edition of
                NO MAN IS AN ISLAND.

1. Merton used the word "not" in his original typescript for the preface. It was mistakenly omitted from the mimeograph version. He corrected one mimeograph version and the word "not" appears in the Vietnamese edition. The version in *Thomas Merton on Peace*, obviously taken from an uncorrected mimeograph copy, omits the word "not."

2. The sentence in the Vietnamese edition reads: "Death becomes a huge, inscrutable and mass-produced *quantity.*"

3. This sentence reads: "They are the principles derived from centuries of religious wisdom which, in the present case, is Christian."

4. In the Vietnamese edition the sentence reads: "And his judgments are distorted by this untruth."

Thomas Merton's
Introductions East & West
has been type-set in 11 Janson
by Open Studio and printed on 70 # Book Natural
by Inter-Collegiate Press. Alan Brilliant designed the book
and bound the cloth edition in Holliston Mills' woven denim Sailcloth.

THE ABBEY OF GETHSEMANI, where these Introductions (or Prefaces) were written, Merton described as "a community of contemplative monks of the Cistercian Order (Trappists), famous for its dedication to silence, manual labor, solitude, meditation and liturgical worship. The Abbey was founded in Kentucky in 1848 by monks from France . . . . The monks observe the Rule of St. Benedict in its strict interpretation and do not engage in teaching or preaching, though in some exceptional cases they write books."

ROBERT EDWARD DAGGY was born in New Castle, Indiana. He is a graduate of Yale University, Columbia University, and the University of Wisconsin-Madison. Since 1974 he has been curator and director of the Thomas Merton Studies Center at Bellarmine College, the repository of Merton's literary estate. He has written several articles on Merton and is currently working on a complete bibliography tentatively entitled *Annotated Merton*. He lives in "Old Louisville" where he is restoring a twelve room house built in 1892.

HARRY JAMES CARGAS, Professor of Literature and Language and Professor of Religion at Webster College in St. Louis, and founder of the literary magazine, *Webster Review*, is the author of nineteen books, including *Harry James Cargas in Conversation with Elie Wiesel*. He was the editor of *The Queen's Work* when Thomas Merton wrote his first preface for a foreign edition which Cargas published, in English, in that magazine. In 1979 Professor Cargas was appointed by President Carter to the United States Holocaust Memorial Council.